TO PLANNING FOR AND LIVING IN
RETIREMENT

NAVIGATING SOCIAL SECURITY,
MEDICARE AND SUPPLEMENTAL INSURANCE,
LONG-TERM CARE, IRA, LIFE INSURANCE,
POST-RETIREMENT INVESTMENT AND INCOME TAXES

Cardinal, an adjective—"of the greatest importance; fundamental"
Synonyms: fundamental, basic, main, chief, primary, crucial, pivotal, prime, principal, paramount, preeminent, highest, key, essential.

- When do I start my Social Security check?
- How do I supplement Medicare?
- Should I purchase Long-Term Care Insurance?
- What should I do with my IRA or 401(k)?
- Am I investing and creating enough income in retirement?
- What about income taxes after age 65?
- How do I handle life insurance and transferring assets to children and grandchildren?
- How do I choose financial and legal professionals to help me?

THE COMPLETE CARDINAL GUIDE TO PLANNING FOR AND LIVING IN RETIREMENT

NAVIGATING SOCIAL SECURITY,
MEDICARE AND SUPPLEMENTAL INSURANCE,
LONG-TERM CARE, IRA, LIFE INSURANCE,
POST-RETIREMENT INVESTMENT AND INCOME TAXES

Hans Scheil

Leapfolio

An imprint of Tupelo Press
North Adams, Massachusetts

Names: Scheil, Hans, author.
Title: The complete Cardinal guide to planning for and living in retirement :
    navigating social security, Medicare and supplemental insurance, long term
    care, IRA, life insurance, post-retirement investment and income taxes /
    Hans Scheil.
Description: First paperback edition. | North Adams, Massachusetts : Tupelo
    Press, [2016] | Includes index.
Identifiers: LCCN 2015046796 | ISBN 9781936797813 (alk. paper)
Subjects: LCSH: Retirement--United States--Planning. | Retirement
    income--United States--Planning. | Older people--Long-term care--United
    States--Planning. | Estate planning--United States. | Tax planning--United
    States.
Classification: LCC HQ1063.2.U6 S39387 2016 | DDC 646.7/90973--dc23
LC record available at http://lccn.loc.gov/2015046796

[ISBN: 978-1-936797-81-3]

Cover and text designed by Hadley Kincade.

First paperback edition: February 2016.

Leapfolio, an imprint of Tupelo Press
Post Office Box 1767
North Adams, Massachusetts 01247
Telephone: (413) 664–9611
editor@tupelopress.org

www.tupelopress.org

CONTENTS

| # THE CARDINAL RETIREMENT PLANNING WAY

Why I've Written This Book

In my practice of retirement planning, I meet with people turning 65 years old every day and find many of them ill prepared for what is in front of them. I meet with clients age 70, 75, or even 80 who have never put their personal affairs in order. Many are ashamed, scared, and think it is too late to start planning. *Wrong*—it is never too late for sound retirement planning! And the sooner you begin, the more likely it is that you will be able to avoid having to make important challenging decisions in the midst of a crisis. A significant part of my practice is crisis planning for clients who are just checking in to an assisted living facility. Their adult children are desperate for leadership through the financial and nursing care maze they have been thrust into. I have the difficult conversations about and with Mom and Dad. I get great satisfaction and joy from helping families navigate this maze.

———◆———

This book is not a do-it-yourself manual for retirement planning. Instead, it outlines the major problems that retirees face and explains simple strategies you can put in place now, with the help of professionals, to make your retirement financially successful. The book covers the range of choices you face with Social Security, Medicare, long-term care, managing and distributing your IRA (Individual Retirement Account), living off your savings and Social Security check, paying and postponing

SUMMARY: THE CARDINAL RETIREMENT PLANNING WAY

- I have been working with age 65+ clients my entire adult life, almost 40 years. People don't change much, and that's a good thing.

- My core values are individual responsibility, the importance of personal growth, conscious decision making, open and honest communication, and the Golden Rule. I look for clients who share these values.

- My family has a lot of personal experience with long-term care. I was a caregiver for my mom, dad, and grandma.

- Remaining independent of the big insurance companies and large financial institutions is the best way for me to offer unbiased fiduciary advice that is really helpful to my clients.

- Don't try eldercare planning and retirement planning on your own. Engage a competent and trustworthy advisor.

taxes, and transferring your wealth to your children and grandchildren. **Please don't try to do eldercare and retirement planning on your own. I strongly encourage you to engage competent, trustworthy advisors every step of the way**. The final chapter explains how to find and choose good advisors.

I aspire to live by my core values and look for matching values in the people I work and consult with. I believe in **individual responsibility**, so I look for clients who believe their financial situation in retirement is their personal responsibility and then I help them achieve their goals. As a CFP® (Certified Financial Planner™) and a fee-based financial advisor, I have a fiduciary responsibility to lead clients to the financial choices that are best for them.

Open and honest communication is another core value for me, and that means clients hear about both the good and the bad in all our dealings. I don't smooth over difficult subjects like sickness, incapacity, aging, and death. In fact, I look for clients who come to trust me enough to share their vulnerabilities. I also believe that experiencing some **discomfort** is necessary for change, personal growth, and planning. Eldercare and retirement planning involve a lot of discomfort—they deal with some very difficult subjects. Finally, **I believe in treating all people like people** and not objects or vehicles for my own fulfillment, and I expect the same **respect** from my clients.

These principles ensure that I can work with clients in an atmosphere of mutual trust and respect, and together we can effectively and successfully explore the financial planning process for retirement. In my experience, many people make financial and insurance decisions from a place of fear, embarrassment, disappointment, loneliness, or sadness. While I acknowledge and validate these difficult emotions, I also work to identify a person's hopes and dreams for themselves and their family. Then we work together to apply some logic and planning to their financial decisions.

You might think you are too young to be reading this book. Not so. If you are under 55, read it for your parents or in-laws. Consider looking into their situation and, if what you read here makes sense to you, send them a copy. I wrote this book to help people.

My Story

My family history isn't all that unusual. But one thing that stands out, which has shaped my own life and work, is our experiences with eldercare and assisted living. I want to tell you these stories because they underscore commonalities that most of us share. So many people don't anticipate having these experiences and are unprepared when they happen. My goal is to encourage you to think ahead and plan for the future.

My dad was an immigrant from Germany who arrived in the United States in 1949. He was able to enter the country by buying a sponsorship from a willing

Hans Scheil.

American. He quickly enlisted in the U.S. Army and was shipped out to Guam. My mom grew up in North Dakota and became a Navy nurse. They met in Guam and were married there in 1951. My dad started selling health insurance part-time in 1952 while attending medical school on the GI Bill. He never finished medical school and went on to become an insurance executive. My parents had five children: Kathy, Margot, Audrey, Johnny, and Jimmy.

My maternal grandma was a teacher and nomad who taught and tutored high school math all over the country. She was a real free spirit. In her mid-70s she started behaving erratically and married an old woodsman who abused her. At age 19, I drove to the area where she was living, coaxed grandma into my car, and essentially kidnapped her. I took her to my mom so she could care for her. Grandma was diagnosed with "hardening of the arteries," what we now know as Alzheimer's disease, and spent her last five years living in a nursing home. Thankfully they cared for her well. I went to visit her weekly. My dad managed her savings account and Social Security check to pay the nursing home bills, so effectively that she died with a little bit of money left.

My grandfather was a World War I veteran and was sick with Parkinson's disease most of his adult life. Grandma left him when my mom was very young. Grandpa lived out his last years in a nursing home for veterans in South Dakota. I am sure he was sad and lonely living hundreds of miles from his family members in Minnesota and Iowa.

Mary Ketter (Grandma).

A nursing home for veterans in a distant state must have been a tough place to live from 1945 to 1966. The government paid the bill for his care and we are thankful for that. He passed away from choking when he was too proud to ask for help cutting his food at a Knights of Columbus banquet. Today, help with eating is one of the six activities of daily living mandated by modern long-term care standards. If he could have received this care at the banquet, he might have lived many more years. I remember my dad telling me about the 21-gun salute and the honor guard playing "Taps" at his graveside service.

Hans and Mary Scheil at their wedding.

My great-grandfather, Patrick McClernan, practiced law well into his 80s and lived to 97. He suffered from the same "hardening of the arteries" as my Grandma, and spent his last years being cared for by The Little Sisters of the Poor in St. Paul, Minnesota. Patrick experienced long-term care in the 1950s. None of his three daughters were able to care for him on a permanent basis. My father transported Patrick in a makeshift ambulance, removing the passenger-side front seat in his car and creating a bed through to the back seat. My mom cared for her grandfather during the ride, sitting behind my dad in the back. This was ten years before Medicare started, so I am sure he had no insurance and few resources to provide for his care.

Between Christmas and New Year's in late 1997, my dad had a severe stroke

Patrick McClernan, in the middle.

that forced him to stay at the University of North Carolina hospital for three weeks. He was such a difficult patient that the nurses had to strap him into a chair. When the nurses wouldn't respond to his repeated use of the call buzzer, he hopped his way into the hall strapped into the chair. We drove him from North Carolina back to Florida, stopping at most of the public bathrooms along Interstate 95. I cleaned the stalls before he went in while my mom waited outside with him. He had no long-term care insurance, despite my attempts to sell it to him over the years and his own lifelong career as an insurance man! I worried about how we were going to pay for his long-term care. We were preparing for years of home health care in Florida provided mostly by my mother and my sister Margot, both registered nurses. I'm sure the thought of being incapacitated and possibly spending time in a nursing home caused him to give up. He died right after Easter in 1998. He was my mentor, and I think about him every day.

I stayed in Florida with my mom for a few days after the funeral, and began helping her prepare financially for what could be many years as a widow living on a smaller amount of Social Security and pension money. I wrote her a small long-term care insurance policy and paid for it myself, though she later took over the premiums. I invested Mommy's money in Certificates of Deposit (CDs) and annuities. She bought a nice townhouse with some of the money from my dad's life insurance policy.

In 2004 Mommy began to forget things. Margot had her tested and we learned she had Alzheimer's, just like her mother and grandfather. She did very well for several

Hans as an older man.

years, aided by some experimental medicines. Even at 80, my mom was caring for "old" people, like her friend Betty whom she described as an "invalid." Mommy drove Betty to church and the grocery store for years. Betty needed help getting in and out of the car, but she had the advantage of actually knowing and remembering where they were going. Mommy could drive just fine, but couldn't go on a trip alone because she needed a navigator. They were a great team!

Hans and Mary, with (left to right) Margot, Jimmy, Kathy, Johnny, and Audrey.

One morning in January of 2011, my sister Margot, the nurse practitioner, had a brain aneurysm and passed away suddenly at age 57. She had no life insurance. The doctors told us that had she survived, she would have lived in a nursing home with 24-hour care for the rest of her life. Margot lived just a few miles from my mom in Florida, while the rest of us siblings live in North Carolina. None of us knew that my mom couldn't live alone until we each took a week at a time living with her after Margot's funeral. She really could not be left alone, but she didn't want to move. Her doctor finally convinced the 87-year-old RN that she needed to move closer to her adult children.

In March 2011 we moved Mommy into an elegant independent living facility in Cary, North Carolina, where she would be surrounded by her four living children. With the help of some financial and legal professionals, she was able to qualify for Veterans Aid and Attendance benefits to the tune of $1,788 per month. Thank you to the Veterans Administration and the US government! In February 2012, she was kicked out of that facility due to a wandering incident and a fall. We quickly moved Mommy a mile down the road to a very nice assisted-living facility. There we discovered that all the window dressing of the elegant facilities was meant to impress us, the kids. Assisted-living residents themselves tend to evaluate the facility by the quality of care they receive from the staff, not by the beauty of the decor or the gourmet food.

In June 2012 we moved Mommy again to another assisted-living facility with a special unit for dementia that allowed the residents to come and go, with light supervision.

After six months there, she was kicked upstairs to the memory unit, with locked doors. The staff at that level of care was great, for the most part—there just were not enough of them. At least one of us four kids was in to see our mom every day. I really enjoyed seeing my mom light up when we visited, but every time I experienced a mix of joy, anger, fear, sadness, and shame. I think that's pretty typical with Alzheimer's.

Mary Scheil (Mom).

In December 2013 we moved our mom to a family-care home with only four residents. We made this move because her care in the memory unit of the assisted-living facility was lacking, and because the cost was being increased from $7,500 per month to over $10,000 due to the management of incontinence. The family-care home cost $5,500 per month, which we paid out of the veterans benefit plus her income and resources. She received the best care in this small facility. Her long-term care insurance was exhausted in the fall of 2013. At 90 years old, she had enjoyed a long and productive life. Never once did she complain. It made me very sad to see such an intelligent and vibrant lady brought down by Alzheimer's over ten years. We could still see an occasional smile and some dry wit through the confusion and weakness right up until the end. Mary Scheil passed away in October 2014.

Four generations suffering from Alzheimer's and dementia, Parkinson's, and circulatory diseases causing strokes and aneurysms. **The purpose of telling this story of my family is to say that you and your family will probably need long-term health care**. And when you do, you'll be happier and less stressed out if you have sufficient financial resources to consider options and make choices. I make my living helping my clients prepare financially for an enjoyable and safe retirement. The long-term care story of my family, and specifically my mother, has forever changed the way I deliver financial planning to my clients. A well-thought-out and well-executed financial plan is crucial. The implications for long-term care of the financial planning strategies I discuss are a central thread throughout this book.

Another underlying theme of the book is this observation: **Regardless of your politics, your wealth, your class or educational status, and your health, the older you get, the more dependent you become on government policies and institutions**. Medicare, Social Security, possibly Medicaid, IRS rules for distributing your IRA, the Veterans Administration, and tax policies will shape the financial landscape of your retirement. You paid into the system for years, now it's your turn to collect. **This book will outline the major problems that retirees face and explain simple strategies you can put in place now, with the help of professionals, to make your retirement financially successful.**

"Both my daughter and son-in-law are very sick. I want to pay for four years of college for my two grandsons."

"I have two military pensions with no survivor benefits. My wife and I built a new house two years ago and mortgaged it. I am 77 with some health problems. If I die first, I want to make sure she can still live here."

"My husband and I have kids from prior marriages. We both want to leave money for each other. We also want to make sure the kids and grandkids receive an inheritance after the second of us goes."

"We want to travel the country in our recreational vehicle; I am worried about my investments supporting me for the rest of my life."

"I always handled the money and want to as long as I can. I would like to make sure our affairs are in order in case I get sick or go first."

"I don't want to be a burden to my children and grandchildren. If I need care, I want to stay in my home as long as I can."

These are all requests made by clients in my financial planning practice. They exemplify the kinds of desires for retirement that are shared by millions of Americans, perhaps by you and your family. I define **Cardinal Retirement as having enough money to live comfortably in retirement while using that money to accomplish your most important goals. It also means preparing financially for sickness, incapacity, and final expenses, and to protect and support the people you choose as your heirs**.

I sold my first Medicare Supplement policy in 1976 at 18 years old in Minneapolis, Minnesota. I worked part time selling Medicare Supplement insurance throughout my college years. More than once, I drove out on the ice in my car to an ice fishing house to sell a policy. A woman opened her door buck naked once; she thought I was someone else! She put on a bathrobe, invited me in, and bought a policy.

In December 1980 I moved to Winston-Salem, North Carolina, to open a new insurance agency selling Medicare Supplements. I had never been to North Carolina, did not know anyone there, and had no agents or existing customers. I was scared out of my mind. But I met many friendly people, worked hard, and launched what has become a successful and gratifying career helping people understand the complexities of retirement planning. I also met my wife, Ronda, while working in Charlotte, and we married in 1985.

Hans Scheil Jr. and Hans Sr.

In 1990 I earned the Chartered Life Underwriter (CLU®) designation and in 1991 the Chartered Financial Consultant (ChFC®) designation. In 1992, I left the small company I had worked for since 1976 to become the Charlotte agency manager for a much larger company that had more to offer my clients, including long-term care insurance. I was starting from scratch again but enabling Ronda to move closer to her family. I obtained my securities registration in 1997 and began offering investment planning to my Medicare clients.

In 2003, the large insurance company I worked for was emerging from bankruptcy. The new executives did not know much about selling insurance or managing sales agents. I had built the largest agency in their company. They made me an offer I couldn't refuse, so I began commuting to Chicago from Charlotte and traveling extensively around the country. I was under extreme stress, very lonely, and sleep deprived, and consequently I had a nervous breakdown in 2007. I knew I needed to make some changes in my lifestyle, so I decided to start over again by appointing myself agency manager in Raleigh, North Carolina. I was out seeing clients again, recruiting and training agents, but this time taking a realistic look at selling for only one company. However, it became clear that selling for only one company was not serving my clients well. During this time I did the work to pass the Certified Financial Planner exam and achieve CFP® designation.

Hans Scheil Jr.

In March 2010 I opened Cardinal, an independent agency offering Medicare Supplement insurance from fifteen different companies. This means that my clients can choose from a wide range of insurance plans. We gradually branched out from North Carolina and now serve a nationwide clientele. In February 2013 I started Cardinal Retirement Planning, chartered as an independent financial planning firm to be free from the supervision of a big investment company. I am free to recommend any and all appropriate investments, thereby putting my clients' interests ahead of Cardinal's and my own. We don't have the overhead of the big firms in either the insurance agency or the investment and financial planning firm. Both firms are rooted in the core values of **personal responsibility, honesty, the importance of personal growth and development, value-conscious choices, independence, and the Golden Rule** ("treat others as you would be treated," not "he who has the gold rules"). This book describes how I help my clients enjoy a Cardinal retirement.

Much of what I've written is most appropriate for people in the middle class financially, but the advice applies to people with low incomes and to wealthy people as well. Medicare and Social Security basically work the same for everyone, whether you're rich, poor, or in between. At Cardinal, we do financial planning *pro bono* for clients age 65 or older who have less than $250,000 in assets. Throughout the book, information that is most relevant for lower-income people is indicated with the symbol **$**, and information that mostly applies to upper-middle-income and affluent clients is indicated by with **$$$$$**.

SUMMARY: THE CARDINAL RETIREMENT PLANNING WAY

- I have been working with age 65+ clients my entire adult life, almost 40 years. People don't change much, and that's a good thing.

- My core values are individual responsibility, the importance of personal growth, conscious decision making, open and honest communication, and the Golden Rule. I look for clients who share these values.

- My family has a lot of personal experience with long-term care. I was a caregiver for my mom, dad, and grandma.

- Remaining independent of the big insurance companies and large financial institutions is the best way for me to offer unbiased fiduciary advice that is really helpful to my clients.

- Don't try eldercare planning and retirement planning on your own. Engage a competent and trustworthy advisor.

CHAPTER 2 | **STRATEGIZING YOUR SOCIAL SECURITY BENEFITS**

S ocial Security was created 80 years ago as a system of government support for Americans in retirement. Here is what President Franklin D. Roosevelt said about Social Security when the program was enacted into law on August 14, 1935:

> We can never insure one hundred percent of the population against one hundred percent of the hazards and vicissitudes of life. But we have tried to frame a law which will give some measure of protection to the average citizen and to his family against the loss of a job and against poverty-ridden old age. This law, too, represents a cornerstone in a structure which is being built, but is by no means complete.... It is ... a law that will take care of human needs and at the same time provide for the United States an economic structure of vastly greater soundness.

Social Security has expanded over the years to include other programs, but for the purposes of this book we are concerned with retirement benefits.

———•———

The first Baby Boomers (people born between 1945 and 1964) started collecting Social Security checks in January 2008 and became eligible for Medicare in January 2011 (Medicare, covered in detail in the next chapter, is our government-sponsored health insurance system for people in retirement; it was created fifty years ago, in

SUMMARY: STRATEGIZING YOUR
SOCIAL SECURITY BENEFITS

- You can start collecting reduced Social Security benefits as early as age 62. Full Retirement Age, when you are entitled to full Social Security benefits, is currently age 66. (It will be increasing to 67 for people born in 1960 or after.) But you can delay starting Social Security until age 70. The longer you hold off, the larger your monthly payments will be.

- Spousal benefits and spousal survivor benefits are affected by the age at which the primary earner starts receiving benefits.

- You will pay income taxes on your Social Security check if your other income exceeds certain levels.

- If your household relies on two Social Security checks, when the first one of you dies, the survivor will continue receiving the larger of the two checks, and the smaller payment goes away. You can plan to compensate for this income reduction with investments, annuities, or life insurance.

- Social Security planning has long-term care implications. Social Security is the base income used to pay the long-term care bill, and any remaining balance must be made up from other income if you are paying the bill yourself.

- Seek help from a financial planner regarding your Social Security decisions. Don't rely on your local Social Security office to guide your decisions. Hire a professional.

1966.) These two programs are a big part of the federal budget, and for that reason they generate political rhetoric that makes headlines and both scares retirees and makes them very mad. I stay out of politics and just try to help my clients make good decisions about when to start receiving Social Security and when and how to sign up for Medicare. I will say this: Don't pay attention to the inflammatory headlines. Medicare and Social Security are too well established and our country is too invested in them for our political and legislative leaders to put an end to either program. No politician wants to be on the wrong side of the powerful lobby of America's retired people.

Franklin D. Roosevelt.

Many people think you start collecting Social Security benefits when you turn 65, but you can actually start at 62 if you're willing to take a smaller amount, and even much earlier than 62 if you become disabled and you have enough quarter-years in your work history. While for most people Medicare starts at age 65, it can be awarded earlier after someone qualifies for Social Security disability, depending on the illness. Most people hire an attorney specializing in Social Security claims when they think they might qualify. I am not an expert on Social Security disability, so this book will focus on your choice of a date to start receiving Social Security. The answer lies somewhere between age 62 and age 70. If both you and your spouse are already collecting Social Security, you might want to skip ahead to the next chapter about Medicare.

I have included a copy of my personal Social Security earnings report in appendix A. You can get your own report online at www.socialsecurity.gov. At Cardinal, we gather the personal Social Security report for all new clients. My report tells me I can draw $1,842 monthly at age 62, $2,570 monthly if I wait until my full retirement age of 66 and 8 months, and $3,255 if I wait until age 70 (the longest I can delay). For me, drawing Social Security before 66 + 8 months has a catch: I have to be retired. If I draw early and earn more than $14,000 of work income in a year, I have to start giving back some or even all of the $1,842 I am collecting monthly. If I am earning less than $14,000 from a job and my chances of living a long time are diminished by my health, it would probably make financial sense to file early and take the money. In that case, there is $81,048 on the table: $1,842 x 44 months (the time between age 62 and age 66 + 8 months). Not until I am somewhere in my late 70s would starting Social Security early cost me money. These alternative scenarios can be very confusing and it is important that you get it right. Don't use my situation to drive your decision—get professional help.

A further complication is that the example above ignores the fact that my wife Ronda's Social Security income is connected to mine. Ignoring Ronda is not a good idea if you are a husband or a financial planner—and I'm both. Ronda's occupation during her prime income-earning years was "Mother." Because she spent the child-rearing years taking care of our two sons, she will be filing under my Social Security account. If I take Social Security early at age 62, I will forever diminish her benefit. But she

FILING STRATEGIES YOU MAY NOT HAVE HEARD ABOUT

$$$$$ File and Suspend: Under this strategy, an individual who is at least at full retirement age (66 if born between 1943 and 1954, 66 + 8 months if born after 1954) files for his or her own retirement benefits and then immediately suspends receipt of them. This sets a filing date for the individual, and initiates the payment of dependent or auxiliary benefits (such as spousal or children's benefits) that are based upon that individual's record. In addition, since the receipt of benefits has been suspended, this individual's future benefit is allowed to grow at the rate of 8% per year, up to his or her age 70.

$$$$$ Restricted Application: Under this strategy, an individual who is at least full retirement age, has not filed for any benefits previously, and whose spouse has established a filing date (and could have suspended), files for ONLY the spousal benefit that is based upon the spouse's record. If the individual doesn't specifically file a Restricted Application, he or she will be filing for all benefits currently available to him or her. "File and suspend" and "restricted application" are potentially being eliminated by the federal budget bill of 2015.

"File and Suspend" and "Restricted Application" are changing as this book is being published. Check with PlanWithCardinal.com for updates.

is the one who is more likely to live into her 90s. While I am alive, she will draw an amount equal to 50% of my benefit. When I die, she will start drawing 100% of my check, foregoing hers. However, if your spouse has a full earning record and a benefit similar or close to yours, then depending on when you retire, spousal benefits are not an issue. None of us knows when we are going to die; we can only plan for what we expect. Life insurance—which can replace lost Social Security income when a spouse dies—is a great planning tool in case things don't work out as expected.

It gets even more complicated. Remember the George Strait song, "All My Ex's Live in Texas"? Well, one's spousal situation, either current and/or former, affects the choice of when is the best time to file. If you were married for ten years or more, no matter how long ago, you can collect on your ex-spouse's Social Security if it will benefit you (unless you remarry). There is no cost to her or him. For example, my client Nick has three women each drawing 50% of his benefit. His current wife plus two ex-wives are all collecting. When Nick dies, two ex-wives and one widow will share his full benefit.

You also need to know about a strategy called "file and suspend." They don't tell you about the "file and suspend" or "restricted application" options down at the Social Security office. But this is the choice that Ronda and I will most likely make. I will still be working at 66 + 8 months. At that point I will file and suspend my benefit, thereby enabling Ronda to start collecting 50% of it, or $1,285 monthly. (Ronda has a small amount of her own Social Security because she has worked some over the years. She can only take my 50% benefit if it's larger than her own benefit.) Meanwhile, my benefit will keep increasing to $3,255 while I am still serving clients

---

SUMMARY: STRATEGIZING YOUR SOCIAL SECURITY BENEFITS

- You can start collecting reduced Social Security benefits as early as age 62. Full Retirement Age, when you are entitled to full Social Security benefits, is currently age 66. (It will be increasing to 67 for people born in 1960 or after.) But you can delay starting Social Security until age 70. The longer you hold off, the larger your monthly payments will be.

- Spousal benefits and spousal survivor benefits are affected by the age at which the primary earner starts receiving benefits.

- You will pay income taxes on your Social Security check if your other income exceeds certain levels.

- If your household relies on two Social Security checks, when the first one of you dies, the survivor will continue receiving the larger of the two checks, and the smaller payment goes away. You can plan to compensate for this income reduction with investments, annuities, or life insurance.

- Social Security planning has long-term care implications. Social Security is the base income used to pay the long-term care bill, and any remaining balance must be made up from other income if you are paying the bill yourself.

- Seek help from a financial planner regarding your Social Security decisions. Don't rely on your local Social Security office to guide your decisions. Hire a professional.

and writing books. I'll start collecting the $3,255 at age 70, and when I die, Ronda will collect the $3,255 for the rest of her life. See, this stuff is confusing—that's why I strongly suggest that you seek professional help.

Pay Attention to the Details!

Robert is 68 and just retired from a long career as a software executive. He and his wife, Sarah, age 61, have two children: a 17-year-old daughter who is a rising senior in high school, and a 22-year-old son with a serious disability and an uncertain future who lives at home and attends college part time. Robert and Sarah are concerned about paying for college for both children and possibly supporting their son long term. Robert deferred his Social Security past age 66 because he didn't need the money while still working and he knew the amount would increase. Sarah is not currently working, but at 61 she is too young to collect Social Security, and if she starts it at 62 her lifetime benefit will diminish. Robert planned to wait until age 70 to start drawing his Social Security—until he hired us to do a financial plan for him.

Our plan showed that Robert is eligible for $3,000 per month from Social Security right now. Once he files for that, he qualifies for one year of $1,300 monthly payments for his daughter. He also possibly qualifies for a benefit for his 22-year-old disabled son, but because of the cap on dependent benefits, we will wait to apply for that until his daughter graduates from high school. When Sarah turns 62, she will file for 50% of Robert's benefit and allow hers to keep growing in the background. Robert and Sarah will be collecting $54,000 or more in Social Security benefits, with only half of it subject to income tax. Had Robert found us two years ago, he could have collected Social Security at his normal retirement age and collected two additional years for his daughter. That $31,000 of lost Social Security for his daughter can never be made up. Even so, Robert's not complaining.

Because much of the generic advice you can find on your own isn't comprehensive, it's all too easy to focus on one decision—like delaying your benefits until you turn 70—but miss something else important. **Don't try Social Security planning at home—get professional help!** Cardinal subscribes to software that runs all the numbers. A full Social Security analysis plus recommendations is just one part of a package of services we provide for a $500 fee.

CHAPTER 3 | **MEDICARE:**
EXCELLENT HEALTH INSURANCE,
BUT IT'S NOT LONG-TERM CARE

Medicare is the government-sponsored health insurance you receive starting the first of the month you turn 65 years old. You need to sign up for it, which you can do by calling 1-800-MEDICARE or **1-800-633-4227**. We help many clients make this phone call. When Medicare, which observed its 50th birthday in 2014, was enacted into law on February 9, 1964, President Lyndon B. Johnson said: "One of the most urgent orders of business at this time is the enactment of hospital insurance for the aged through Social Security to help older people meet the high costs of illness without jeopardizing their economic independence."

———◆———

Part A of Medicare is your **hospital insurance**. There is no monthly cost to you for Part A and therefore no reason to delay signing up for it when you turn 65. Part B of Medicare covers **doctors and outpatient services**. Part B can start at the same time as Part A, and most people do this. The monthly cost for Part B is $104.90, unless you are deemed "higher income" by Medicare (more on that below). Part B charges can be deducted right out of your Social Security check. However, if you are still working and covered by group insurance, you can and should delay your enrollment in Medicare Part B (and D as well). Part C of Medicare, also called Medicare Advantage, lets you choose to receive your benefits from a private insurance company instead of directly from the government. Part D of Medicare covers prescription drugs and must be purchased through a private insurance company. You can

SUMMARY: MEDICARE STRATEGIZING

- [...]e Part A and Part B start (for most people) on the first of [...] month before their 65th birthday. Part A is free and Part B has a monthly cost. If you are still working at 65 and covered by group insurance, sign up for A at 65 and delay enrolling in B until you retire.

- Choose a Medicare Advantage plan (Parts C and D) if you want no or a low insurance premium, deductibles, and copayments, and don't mind the insurance company choosing your doctors and hospitals for you. Choose a Medicare Supplement Plan G or F plus a separate Part D plan if you want low or no deductibles and no copayments, plus you want the freedom to go to any doctor or hospital that takes Medicare.

- Buy Part D after your agent has entered your prescriptions and preferred pharmacy into Medicare.gov and run a comparison of plans.

- Buy your Medicare Supplement Plan G or F from an independent agent who does not have a vested interest in steering you to one company. Look at a premium comparison report before you buy: see PlanWithCardinal.com.

- If you have been on a Medicare Supplement plan for a few years, you are probably paying too much. Shop around using a Medicare Supplement premium comparison report at PlanWithCardinal.com.

- $ If you qualify for LIS (the low-income subsidy program) or Extra Help, the government will pay your Part B premium for you and reduce your Part D drug copayments.

- $$$$$ Prepare to pay higher-income surcharges for Medicare Parts B and D if your income is over $85,000 as a single person or $170,000 as a couple.

- Long-term care implication of Medicare: Don't rely on Medicare to pay your long-term care bill. It doesn't!

enroll in Part C and Part D around your 65th birthday, and then each fall you can change your plan during a specific period called open enrollment. You'll know that Medicare Advantage open enrollment season is around the corner when all those annoying commercials start showing up on TV. You know, the ones with 58-year-old actors dressed and made up to look like 70-year-olds who "look real good for their age." As with Medicare Part B, if you are still working and covered by group insurance, it's probably advisable to delay your enrollment in Part D.

When we consult with clients about their Medicare coverage, we take two major factors into consideration: Do they want to choose their own doctors and hospitals; and are they willing to pay the Medicare Supplement premiums that will enable them to make those choices? The answers to these questions will go a long way toward determining what Medicare coverage decisions are in their best interest. We'll discuss the elements of Medicare in greater detail and illustrate some of them with stories of real Cardinal clients.

Lyndon B. Johnson.

How Medicare Works

Megan and Jason live in a small Southern town not far from the coast. Jason worked in management and Megan in bookkeeping at the local manufacturing facility. Not only did the factory close at the end of Jason's career, but the management group lost most of his pension money. Megan and Jason have lived modestly off of their Social Security checks for eighteen years. Both have great attitudes and are optimistic people. Then Jason had a medical emergency.

Medicare Part A covers ALL your hospital costs for the first 60 days, minus a deductible of $1,260 (in 2015). Jason had a heart attack and a stroke and needed bypass surgery immediately. He was in cardiac care, then intensive care, and next a regular room for a total of twenty-two days. Jason's hospital bill was $212,000. Medicare Part A paid the hospital $210,800. Upon being discharged Jason was immediately transferred to a skilled nursing facility across the street from the hospital. Medicare Part A paid in full Jason's first twenty days there. From day 21 to day 100, Part A paid all costs above $157.50/day, which Jason and Megan had to pay. (In their case, this cost was covered by a Medicare Supplement policy, see below.) Medicare coverage then stops after 100 days. It can stop paying for skilled nursing care before the 100th day if the patient stops improving. But in Jason's case, the full 100 days were covered. **Don't rely on Medicare to pay your long-term care bill.** We'll discuss this point further in the next chapter.

Medicare Part A (Hospital Insurance) helps cover

- Inpatient care in hospitals
- Skilled nursing facility, hospice, and home health care

Medicare Part B (Medical Insurance) helps cover

- Services from doctors and other health-care providers, hospital outpatient care, durable medical equipment, and home health care
- Preventative services to help maintain your health and to keep certain illnesses from getting worse

Medicare Part C (Medicare Advantage)

- Includes all benefits and services covered under Part A and Part B
- Run by Medicare-approved private insurance companies
- Usually includes Medicare prescription drug coverage (Part D) as part of the plan
- May include extra benefits and services for an extra cost

Medicare Part D (Medicare Prescription Drug Coverage)

- Helps cover the cost of outpatient prescription drugs
- Run by Medicare-approved private insurance companies
- May help you lower your prescription drug costs and help protect against higher costs in the future

Medicare Part B (doctor and outpatient coverage) has an annual deductible of only $147 (in 2015). After that, Medicare pays roughly 80% of your doctor and outpatient bills. Jason's Part B charges were $73,000, of which $58,400 was paid by Medicare. Part B is where your biggest liability lies if you do not have proper Medicare Supplement coverage. (Medicare Supplement, described in detail below, is an insurance policy that provides additional coverage beyond the Medicare basics.) **You want to be sure to sign up for Part B on time, usually the first of the month before your 65th birthday**—there are late enrollment penalties, it's hard to enroll later, and late registration affects your open enrollment status for Medicare Supplement.

Part C of Medicare, also known as **Medicare Advantage**, was invented in 2006. Its purpose is for the government to outsource the delivery of your Medicare benefits to a private insurance company. The government pays the insurance company a monthly fee to deliver your benefits. In exchange, the company must provide you with better benefits than were previously available through traditional Medicare. You are also in managed care, so you are required to go to doctors and hospitals on the insurance company's roster. A Part C plan also provides you with Part D prescription drug benefits, so you don't have to pay a Part D monthly premium. **The main benefit of Medicare Advantage is that you avoid paying premiums for a Medicare Supplement and Part D. The big disadvantage is that you lose the ability to pick doctors and hospitals of your choice—costs will be much higher for out-of-network providers.** The drug plan you receive as part of the package may not be the one you would have picked if you bought your Part D plan separately. Cardinal sells policies for most of these Part C Medicare Advantage plans, and we do write them for clients who can't afford or don't want to pay the $1,500 to $2,000 annual premium for a Medicare Supplement policy and Part D drug plan. Much depends on your individual situation, and again I emphasize: **Don't try Medicare planning at home, instead seek professional help.**

Part D of Medicare started in 2005 and, despite the confusion it can cause, it is a blessing for older Americans. Before 2005 there were no drug benefits for Medicare beneficiaries. I helped clients buy drugs from Canada and also wrote to drug companies on behalf of clients asking for help paying for expensive medicines. **Sign up for a Part D plan when you are 65, unless you are still working and covered by group insurance. Sign up even if you are taking few or no drugs now. There are big penalties for signing up for Part D late, and they last the rest of your life.** An online calculator at Medicare.org lets you enter your prescriptions plus pharmacy of choice and then rates all the Medicare Part D plans available you. Every fall of the year you can run this report and change plans if you like. Cardinal provides this service for our clients every year.

Medicare Supplement Plans

I have been selling **Medicare Supplement** insurance for nearly 40 years, and we don't charge for this service. I know it very well! In 1990, the National Association of Insurance Commissioners (NAIC) coordinated with the Center for Medicare Services (CMS) to make sweeping changes in Medicare Supplement insurance. The NAIC standardized policies to make it easier for consumers to compare and contrast. The law also now requires that when a consumer switches insurance companies, the new company must cover any pre-existing conditions under the new policy. Twenty-five years later, it seems like no one outside the industry has noticed this big change. Every day we talk to people who are paying $200 to $300 a month for Medicare Supplement Plan F (the most complete coverage), when they could cut their premiums significantly while keeping exactly the same coverage. Many potential clients just don't believe us. Why is this so? Because most retirees are very happy with their Medicare Supplement even though it costs them an arm and a leg. Between Medicare Parts A and B and the Plan F supplemental coverage, all their hospital

Benefits	Medicare Supplement Insurance (Medigap) Plans									
	A	B	C	D	F	G	K	L	M	N
Medicare Part A and hospital costs (up to an additional 365 days after Medicare benefits are used)	100%	100%	100%	100%	100%	100%	100%	100%	100%	100%
Medicare Part B coinsurance or copayment	100%	100%	100%	100%	100%	100%	50%	75%	100%	100% ★★★
Blood (first 3 pints)	100%	100%	100%	100%	100%	100%	50%	75%	100%	100%
Part A hospice care coinsurance or copayment	100%	100%	100%	100%	100%	100%	50%	75%	100%	100%
Skilled nursing facility care coinsurance			100%	100%	100%	100%	50%	75%	100%	100%
Part A deductible		100%	100%	100%	100%	100%	50%	75%	50%	100%
Part B deductible			100%		100%					
Part B excess charges					100%	100%				
Foreign travel emergency (up to plan limits)			80%	80%	80%	80%			80%	80%

and doctor costs are paid, and paid quickly. Most retirees think the supplement policy pays a larger share of the pie than it actually does. They don't want to rock the boat, so they just keep paying high premiums. I will walk you through the case for shopping your Medicare Supplement policy with an independent agent using the guide printed by NAIC and CMS. You can download a full copy of the 2015 Medicare guide at PlanWithCardinal.com, or contact Medicare and request that a copy be mailed to your house.

The crux of this guide is the list of the only ten Medicare Supplement / Medigap policies that can be sold in your state (page 11 in the 2015 guide). (The situation is different in Minnesota, Wisconsin, and Massachusetts.) That's it—only ten policies are allowed, and the lettered policies are exactly the same from company to company (page 19 in the 2015 guide). According to industry research, 60% of people across the U.S. who own Medicare Supplements have Plan F. Plan F pays all your deductibles and copayments, and even pays excess charges if you go to a doctor who charges more than Medicare approves. Plan G offers the next best comprehensive coverage and is the best value for most people.

Our client Jason from earlier in the chapter has a Plan G policy through Cardinal. At 80 years old, it costs him $130/month. Jason's Plan G paid the $15,800 copayment ($157.50/day) for the skilled nursing facility he used after he left the hospital, which Medicare Part A did not cover—thus leaving Jason with a zero balance due. The **only difference** between Plan F and Plan G is the $147 annual deductible for the latter. But the annual premium for Plan G can be up to $400 less than for Plan F, so it makes sense for most people.

Now that we've narrowed down the Medicare Supplement choices to Plan F or Plan G, let's decide which insurance company to buy it from.

For most of my almost 40 years in the insurance business, it has been pretty hard to get ahold of the Medicare Supplement rates from other companies. Insurance companies like to keep their little calculators very close to the vest. Today, a consulting actuarial company sells rate information to people like me. You can go to my website, PlanWith-Cardinal.com, click on Medicare Supplement, and type in your age, zip code, and smoker status, and the calculator will show you the range of prices for exactly the same coverage from several companies. The entire report for Plans F and G for a married 70-year-old female nonsmoker in zip code 27511 appears in appendix B. Check out the monthly price difference between the lowest and the highest premiums—it costs more than double to have Medicare Supplement insurance with the most expensive company. At Cardinal, we commonly save clients $30, $50, even $100 per month by simply moving them to a different company.

If you have health conditions, some of these companies might not accept you on a new policy, but at Cardinal we know which ones accept which health conditions, so we can steer you in the right direction. Medicare's own publication puts this in black and white: "If you've had your current Medigap policy longer than 6 months and want to replace it with a new one with the same benefits and the insurance company agrees to it, they can't write pre-existing conditions, waiting periods, elimination periods, or probationary periods into the replacement policy" (*Choosing a Medigap Policy: 2015,* page 33). These changes were made clear back in 1990, but most consumers still are not aware that all the policies are the same and there is little risk in changing companies. The Medicare Supplement market is a small industry with a few players controlling the flow of information. **Part of my mission is to get the word out that it pays to shop around for your Medicare Supplement and there is little risk in changing companies.**

Mary Lou came to us considering a change in her Medicare Supplement insurance company. She is an insulin-dependent diabetic and has some lung issues. She could no longer afford her Medicare Supplement premiums and was considering dropping her plan. We lowered her monthly Supplement premium from $186.59 to $132.47, saving her $54.12/month. In addition, the federal government has a program called "Extra Help" or the "Low Income Subsidy" (LIS). Mary Lou had never heard of it. Because her monthly income was under $1,137 and her countable assets (home, personal car, and jewelry don't count) were under $27,250, we were able to help Mary Lou qualify for LIS. The government now pays her $104.90 monthly premium for Part B (in 2015) and she qualifies for reduced copays through her Part D plan. All added up, we saved Mary Lou $300/month and kept her insured. Mary Lou sent us an email of thanks and said the $300 is going toward art supplies and a new Easter dress, her first in years. Helping people like Mary Lou is what brings me a lot of joy in my work. At Cardinal, we serve over 5,000 Medicare Supplement clients; Mary Lou's story is one of too many stories to tell. Each and every one of them matters to me. Most of these clients bought their current policy from us, and their benefits are exactly the same as under their old policy but they're paying $30, $50, even $100 less per month than their previous premium. It pays to shop around. Do your shopping with an **independent** agent who can show you price quotes from every company.

The biggest weakness in the Medicare program for retirees is the lack of coverage for long-term intermediate and custodial care. This is why long-term care insurance is so important. Read the warning about the need for long-term care on page 4 of my personal Social Security statement (appendix A). The same warning is on yours, too!

Social Security, Medicare, and Long-Term Care

It's easy to think that the government programs we've created—Social Security and Medicare—will fully take care of you in your retirement years. But there are limits to the benefits that these programs provide, which is why you need a larger perspective on long-term care. That's the subject of the next chapter. This quote, which you'll find on your own Social Security statement, says it all:

> Social Security pays retirement, disability, family and survivor benefits. Medicare, a separate program run by the Centers for Medicare and Medicaid Services, helps pay for inpatient hospital care, nursing care, doctors' fees, drugs, and other medical services and supplies to people age 65 and older, as well as to people who have been receiving Social Security disability benefits for two years or more. **Medicare does not pay for long-term care, so you may want to consider options for private insurance**. Your Social Security covered earnings qualify you for both programs.

SUMMARY: MEDICARE STRATEGIZING

- Medicare Part A and Part B start (for most people) on the first of the month before their 65th birthday. Part A is free and Part B has a monthly cost. If you are still working at 65 and covered by group insurance, sign up for A at 65 and delay enrolling in B until you retire.

- Choose a Medicare Advantage plan (Parts C and D) if you want no or a low insurance premium, deductibles, and copayments, and don't mind the insurance company choosing your doctors and hospitals for you. Choose a Medicare Supplement Plan G or F plus a separate Part D plan if you want low or no deductibles and no copayments, plus you want the freedom to go to any doctor or hospital that takes Medicare.

- Buy Part D after your agent has entered your prescriptions and preferred pharmacy into Medicare.gov and run a comparison of plans.

- Buy your Medicare Supplement Plan G or F from an independent agent who does not have a vested interest in steering you to one company. Look at a premium comparison report before you buy: see PlanWithCardinal.com.

- If you have been on a Medicare Supplement plan for a few years, you are probably paying too much. Shop around using a Medicare Supplement premium comparison report at PlanWithCardinal.com.

- $ If you qualify for LIS (the low-income subsidy program) or Extra Help, the government will pay your Part B premium for you and reduce your Part D drug copayments.

- $$$$$ Prepare to pay higher-income surcharges for Medicare Parts B and D if your income is over $85,000 as a single person or $170,000 as a couple.

- Long-term care implication of Medicare: Don't rely on Medicare to pay your long-term care bill. It doesn't!

CHAPTER 4 | **LONG-TERM CARE:**
THERE'S AN APPROPRIATE
STRATEGY FOR EVERY FAMILY

This poem, which is very poignant to me, reminds us to always respect the dignity of elders who experience frailty or dementia. And it reflects the inevitable pain we all feel when our loved ones age into challenging circumstances.

Do Not Ask Me to Remember

Do not ask me to remember
Don't try to make me understand,
Let me rest and know you're with me,
Kiss my cheek and hold my hand.
I'm confused beyond your concept,
I am sad and sick and lost.
All I know is that I need you
To be with me at all cost.
Do not lose your patience with me,
Do not scold or curse or cry.
I can't help the way I'm acting,
Can't be different though I try.
Just remember that I need you,
That the best of me is gone,
Please don't fail to stand beside me,
Love me 'til my life is done.

—Author Unknown

I already told you a bit about my Mom and her ten-year struggle with Alzheimer's. The long-term care insurance policy she owned, along with the federal Veterans Aid and Attendance program (see below), made it possible for her to be well cared for in the last four years of her life. She was able to pass on with some dignity and leave a little something to her four surviving children and seven grandchildren. I still miss her very much. Alice Watkins and Dee Dee Harris of the Alzheimer's Association of North Carolina were a big help to our family during Mom's last four years. They counseled us, cried with us, referred us to professional caregivers, and taught us how to care for our mom. None of us know if our life will end like Mary's, but we do have choices in financial planning in case it does. Long-term care planning is just as much for your family and caregivers as it is for you.

SUMMARY: LONG-TERM CARE STRATEGIZING

- You might live a long life, and if you do, you might become frail or memory impaired and end up needing care. The financial consequences of that care can be devastating to your family.

- Long-term care doesn't have to mean a nursing home. It includes home health care, assisted living, and adult day care. More and more, clients are cared for at home with paid assistance coming in to help.

- Financial strategies include short-term care insurance, traditional long-term care insurance, hybrid long-term care insurance, and/or a financial plan for self-insurance. These solutions can be mixed and matched to come up with your personal plan.

- Consider a partnership long-term care policy, which allows you to go on Medicaid and protect some of your assets.

- ($) Medicaid is a last resort to pay for your care.

- Get professional help from an independent insurance agent and a financial professional who specializes in eldercare and long-term care.

- ($$$$$) If you are relatively affluent, there can be tax advantages in planning for long-term care.

To prepare yourself financially for long-term care, I ask you to accept three facts:

1. It is possible you will live to a ripe old age.
2. If you do live to a ripe old age, you might need professional care for several months, or even several years.
3. The financial consequences of your care could be devastating to you and your family.

As a financial advisor and Certified Financial Planner™, I have a fiduciary responsibility to present these facts to every client I consult with. Most people have more difficulty accepting the possibility of incapacity than they do facing the reality of their own death. The biggest consequences of failing to plan for long-term care are suffered by the family. I deal with family members all the time who are doing last-minute planning for a client who has just checked in to a facility or is receiving care at home. I experience the confusion, fear, anxiety, pain, and disappointment that comes with these situations. Our job at Cardinal is to help people avoid or minimize these challenges.

Cardinal's Solutions for Long-Term Care

At Cardinal we offer four solutions to the problem of financial planning for long-term care. These solutions are not mutually exclusive—they can be mixed and matched depending upon your assets, income, and personal preferences. Our basic strategy is to create a $6,000 monthly income for you (in today's dollars) that you start to receive in the future when you need it. Prior to that point at which you need it, you will have other income like Social Security, a pension, and investment earnings you can use to self-insure. For clients who choose to self-insure part or all of the risk, we look carefully at all the income sources and numbers and adjust accordingly.

SELF-INSURANCE means providing the entire $6,000/month yourself from your income and assets. This requires careful planning so your family members will know what to do when and if you start to need outside care. It is much better to have a financial planner doing this work for you now than to have a nursing home administrator doing these calculations when you are being admitted.

We start with your Social Security check and any other income you receive that is reliable. We deduct ongoing monthly expenses that won't go away if you are in a facility. The net number is applied toward the $6,000 and what's left is the monthly dollar amount needed to fill the gap. Then we add up your financial assets and begin paying the gap number out of interest first, principal second. We recommend using your remaining IRA money first, because the assisted living or nursing home bill will give you a big tax deduction as a medical expense. This hit me while doing my Mom's taxes after she was confined. She had $66,000 in medical expense deductions and very little income to deduct it against. We sell annuity products from several different insurance companies that allow you to defer income taxes on current earnings until you draw the money out. (An annuity is a series of payments you receive over a period of time, often specified as for life.) Some of the companies enhance the monthly income available to you if you use it to pay for long-term care. **Self-insurance may be your only option if your health conditions eliminate the next three solutions.**

SHORT-TERM CARE INSURANCE gives your family almost a year of $6,000 monthly payments while they figure out how to make self-insurance work for you. It may not sound like much, but I can tell you that the families who are collecting on it are very grateful for the time it buys them. Short-term care insurance pays for home health care as well as facility care, and you can bank the unused money to make it last longer than a year. A 70-year-old female nonsmoker can buy a $72,000 plan for $101.01 monthly; couples receive a 10% discount. The health criteria are much easier to meet than for traditional long-term policies, which makes short-term care available to more people.

TRADITIONAL LONG-TERM CARE INSURANCE is just what is sounds like: Thinking ahead, you purchase a policy that would pay $6,000 monthly once you need long-term care and lasts for several years up to the policy maximum. Caveat: Such a policy must be purchased well in advance of the foreseeable need. Most companies now offer a maximum of ten years of benefits; we typically sell our clients two to five years, which keeps the premium affordable. The policy pays a benefit for either home health care or facility care and allows you to bank the unused portion, which makes the benefits last longer. I also recommend inflation protection. A 70-year-old female nonsmoker can purchase $6,000/month of benefits for four years with a built-in 3% inflation factor for $730.89 monthly (or $8,120.96 for the discounted annual premium). A plan for a married couple the same age will cost substantially less per person, because male rates are lower than female rates and there is a couples discount.

There are some disadvantages to a traditional long-term care plan. If you pay in to the policy for several years and never use it, all your money has gone to pay other policyholders who needed benefits. The company can raise the premium—with the approval of insurance regulators—perhaps when you are vulnerable and can't afford it. Also, health qualifications for traditional long-term care insurance have become tougher over the years. Underwriting will request records from your doctor and possibly any specialists you have seen, will run a report of your prescriptions, and will do a little memory test that will seem silly over the phone. Some companies even send a nurse to your house to examine you.

HYBRID LONG-TERM CARE is the fastest-growing segment of the long-term care business. Sharing some features of life insurance, hybrid long-term care is more consumer friendly and addresses several of the big problems of traditional long-term care insurance. First, if you don't use it during your lifetime, there is a death benefit that enables your beneficiaries to receive the unused portion when you die. Most of these policies also have a return-of-premium feature that allows you to get all your premiums back (without interest) if you ever want to cancel your insurance. Second, the company can never raise the premium. Third, the money can be used for a variety of care settings, including in-home and rehabilitation care. The trade-off is that you pay for a hybrid policy all up front. The cost is generally $50,000 to $100,000, and one of the companies Cardinal works with lets you use IRA money to fund it. You do have to meet health qualifications, but they are more lenient since you are paying up front.

Several life insurance policies with annual premiums allow you to access the death benefit for long-term care. You need to purchase $300,000 or more of permanent life insurance to receive a benefit sufficient to pay your long-term care bill. Surprisingly, it is easier for people with diabetes or heart conditions to qualify for permanent life insurance policies than for long-term care insurance.

A nifty cost-of-care survey is available on the Genworth website (www.genworth.com/corporate/about-genworth/industry-expertise/cost-of-care.html). You can plug in your city and state and it will show you average costs in your area—it even includes an inflation factor and projects costs into the future. For example, in Raleigh, North Carolina, in 2015, a private room in a skilled nursing home averages $76,650 annually and a semi-private room averages $73,000. Assisted living costs $50,400 and adult day care costs $13,780. A home health aide caring for you in your home 44 hours per week costs about $47,000 a year. These numbers knock a pretty good hole in even the best-thought-out financial plans. **One way or another, Cardinal can figure out an effective financial strategy for protecting you against the cost of long-term care.**

Medicaid and Veterans Aid and Attendance

$ **Medicaid**, which is government assistance, will pay for your long-term care after you have spent down almost all of your money. (If you qualify for Medicaid, it will only pay for long-term care if your assets amount to around $2,000 or less.) If you have to use Medicaid, it is best to enter a facility as a private payer and transition to Medicaid after you have used your own money. Most states have Long-Term Care Partnership (LTCP) programs that allow you to purchase a limited long-term care policy that works in partnership with the state Medicaid program. They allow you to keep some of your assets and still go on Medicaid after your policy has run out of benefits. Partnership programs work best for people with $100,000 to $300,000 in assets (excluding their home). **Veterans Aid and Attendance** provides long-term care benefits for any veteran who served even one day in the military while our country was at war. If you intend to use Medicaid or Veterans Aid and Attendance to pay for your long-term care, you need to do some planning and it is important to be referred to the right professional to help you. Cardinal provides these services, or we can refer you to professionals in your area.

Veterans Aid and Attendance is a program that pays a qualifying veteran $1,788 monthly and a qualifying veteran's spouse or widow $1,149 monthly. To be eligible, a veteran has to have served one day of active duty while the U.S. was at war, be in need of long-term care when applying, and meet income and asset maximums. The VA currently allows an applicant to make financial adjustments the month before applying to bring him or her within the financial guidelines. (This rule might have changed since this book was published.) Regardless, Cardinal can help a vet do financial planning to meet the guidelines. My mom collected the $1,788 monthly for 3 ½ years and we are very thankful she had it.

Our client Michael just received his approval from the VA for $1,788 monthly (see the appendix). Michael had been retired and living in Florida for several years. He was mostly out of touch with his four children since they were young. His second wife divorced him in 2005 and has since passed away. Alcohol abuse played a role in his life. In early 2013, his daughter Christina received a call from someone in Florida saying that her father needed someone in the family to take care of him. She managed to get him moved up to North Carolina and into a facility that could help him.

Michael had not filed his taxes in ten years. His financial accounts were frozen because his mail was returned. Christina was distraught. She couldn't get the financial institutions to speak with her even though she had power of attorney; the accounts were frozen. The answer was to bring Michael into our office. I called the financial institutions, we turned on the speakerphone, and Christina held up flashcards in front of Michael to give them his identifying information. Michael is a veteran and wanted to qualify for Veterans Aid and Attendance. We needed to move the frozen assets into a trust so he could meet the asset minimums. People with dementia who live alone generally leave one heck of a financial mess for their kids to deal with once they take over. Cardinal has become pretty good at helping families dig out of this kind of financial mess.

If you or your spouse is a vet, a qualified advisor can help you look into Veterans Aid and Attendance. A sample letter of approval is in appendix C.

Personal Long-Term Care Stories of Cardinal Clients

Jason and Megan are age 80+ clients you first met in chapter 3. We helped them lower their Medicare Supplement premiums, manage premiums on an old life insurance policy that has an outstanding loan, and refinance some debt they incurred repairing their home. Jason had a heart attack, then a stroke, and is still in recovery. Megan called me in a panic, hurting and very sad, right after Jason went into the hospital. I asked her to tend to Jason's immediate needs and her needs at the moment, and told her we would figure out a plan in a few weeks. My associate phoned Medicaid in their county, and in conjunction with the social worker at the nursing home they are fast-tracking Jason to Medicaid and VA benefits. If Jason and Megan had money in the bank or any investments, Medicaid would require them to spend assets first before putting Jason on Medicaid. Most likely, his Social Security check will go toward paying the nursing home. Megan will now need to live off of her Social Security benefits. We will be in contact with the veterans' advocate in their area to try and qualify Jason for Veterans Aid and Attendance.

Marshall and Elizabeth were clients in their late 70s and both were in excellent health when we met them. They still carried the same Medicare Supplement policies they bought at age 65 and had never looked into changing, because they "paid all our bills." Cardinal was able to cut their Medicare Supplement premium in half pretty easily. Marshall asked us to look at the long-term care insurance he carried with the same company. It started with a premium of $375 a month fourteen years earlier but had grown to cost $1,400 per month. Marshall and Elizabeth also had about $500,000 in IRA accounts and took minimum distributions each year. I showed Marshall a life insurance-annuity combination policy using IRA money that is so unique the company has a patent on it. Marshall and Elizabeth would transfer $180,000 of their IRA money into a survivorship life insurance policy that will pay $250,000 to their children when the second of them dies (providing the kids had not already been advanced that money to pay for their parents' long-term care). Next they would pay $50,000 in a single premium to purchase a lifetime $66,000-per-year long-term care extension rider that includes inflation protection and a guarantee of no premium increases for life, and would pay their three sons $250,000 upon the second death (if they had not already used that money to pay for long-term care). Marshall and Elizabeth bought this policy and canceled their $1,400/month long-term care policy.

Nicole is a 65-year-old who first came to us to buy a Medicare Supplement policy and Part D drug plan. She had married very young, divorced in early middle age, and has been single ever since, with one son in his early 30s. Nicole's mother left her $470,000 in a trust that was structured so Nicole receives the interest earnings and the principal is to go to her son Thomas at her death. The trust was invested in bonds (safe) but was producing very little income for Nicole. I contacted the trustee to find out if Nicole could use the trust principal in the event she needed long-term care and was told no—because that would compromise the principal ultimately owed to her son. I was able to work out an agreement with Thomas that Nicole would take $300,000 from

$$$$$ Tax advantages are offered to purchase long-term care insurance (see the appendix), plus there are tax advantages to a strategy using tax-deferred income to pay for care. Wealthy people often tell me they will just pay for long-term care themselves if they need it. This is a simple solution to a complex problem. Your family will have enough stress to deal with when placing you in care without having to worry about liquidating your investments to pay for it. I can usually engage wealthy clients in a conversation about saving on taxes more easily than I can talk with them about becoming incapacitated.

the trust and buy a single-premium life insurance policy with a death benefit for him of $540,000. If Nicole needs long-term care, she can access the $540,000 at a rate of $15,159.72 per month if she's in a facility, or $9,095.83 per month for home health care. The $300,000 cash value at the insurance company will most likely grow well beyond the guaranteed interest, creating a death benefit of $800,000 to $900,000 if Nicole lives into her 80s or 90s. Thomas immediately received a much-needed check for $149,000 (representing his portion of the settlement of the trust principal). Cardinal was able to figure out a way to provide financial security for both Nicole and her son.

Patricia's son worked for Cardinal as an intern while attending North Carolina State University. He graduated with a degree in Mechanical and Aerospace Engineering and is the only true "rocket scientist" I have ever known. Patricia has been divorced for many years and lives alone. She cared for her mother several years ago and is very concerned about her own long-term care. Patricia has financial assets totaling $65,000. She was a teacher and has both a decent pension and Social Security. She could not afford a large long-term care policy but wanted some protection. We wrote her a partnership policy with a maximum benefit of $3,500 per month at a cost of $186.38 per month (or discounted for annual premiums, $2,070). If she needs long-term care, either at home or in a facility, she can rely on the policy until it pays out the maximum of $84,000. Patricia can then apply for Medicaid, while keeping $84,000 of her financial assets protected.

Sharon, who is 68, purchased a Plan F Medicare Supplement policy from Cardinal for $115 monthly. She had been paying $184.40 monthly for the identical Plan F policy with another company. While we were helping reduce her Medicare Supplement premium, Sharon expressed interest in purchasing long-term care insurance but feared she could not afford it. We took the savings from her Medicare Supplement cost reduction ($184.40 - $115.00 = $69.40) and wrote her a short-term care policy. The policy pays $100/day or $3,000/month, has a maximum of 240 days or $24,000, has a zero day elimination period (comparable to having no deductible), and pays for either home health care or nursing home care. This certainly is not comprehensive coverage, but if you speak to families who go through nursing home admission or home health care, they would be very pleased to have this $24,000 coverage to get them in the door. This type of short-term policy buys some time.

George's stepdaughter, Sue, is the only heir he has left. Sue is doing a very loving job of looking after George since his stroke. George married Sue's mother while Sue was still young. The home he lived in before his stroke belonged to Sue's mother originally. George is a veteran, and Sue needed us to arrange George's income and assets so he could qualify for Veterans Aid and Attendance.

A long-term care solution for people who are over age 74 and already receiving care is now available. It is offered by a large A+ rated insurance company. George is 79 years old and had a major stroke. He is currently receiving care in an assisted-living facility. His stepdaughter, who legally serves as his power of attorney, recently applied

---

SUMMARY: LONG-TERM CARE STRATEGIZING

- You might live a long life, and if you do, you might become frail or memory impaired and end up needing care. The financial consequences of that care can be devastating to your family.

- Long-term care doesn't have to mean a nursing home. It includes home health care, assisted living, and adult day care. More and more, clients are cared for at home with paid assistance coming in to help.

- Financial strategies include short-term care insurance, traditional long-term care insurance, hybrid long-term care insurance, and/or a financial plan for self-insurance. These solutions can be mixed and matched to come up with your personal plan.

- Consider a partnership long-term care policy, which allows you to go on Medicaid and protect some of your assets.

- ($) Medicaid is a last resort to pay for your care.

- Get professional help from an independent insurance agent and a financial professional who specializes in eldercare and long-term care.

- ($$$$$) If you are relatively affluent, there can be tax advantages in planning for long-term care.

for this policy on George's behalf. George had $292,000 in a savings account earning very little interest. The insurance company did what is called reverse underwriting and determined that for that amount of money, they can write a policy to pay him $3,020 monthly for the rest of his life. This income will pay 60% of his assisted-living rent. If George dies in the first two years, the premium will be partially refunded to his heirs. If he lives for fifteen years, the insurance company will pay out a lot more than was paid in. For the right client, this policy is a blessing.

For any client, Cardinal can devise a sound financial strategy to cover the costs of long-term care and reduce the risks to the individual and the family.

| ## ASSETS:
YOUR IRA, 401(K), AND PENSION PLAN

Atraditional **IRA** is an Individual Retirement Account (or sometimes, Arrangement), established in the United States by the Employee Retirement Income Security Act of 1974 (ERISA). The IRA is held at a custodian institution such as a bank or brokerage, and may be invested in anything that the custodian allows—for instance, a bank may allow certificates of deposit, and a brokerage may allow stocks and mutual funds. The key feature of an IRA is that taxes due on the money are deferred until the money is withdrawn. Similarly, a 401(k) is a workplace savings plan that lets employees invest a portion of their paycheck before taxes are taken out. The savings can grow, tax free, until retirement, at which point withdrawals will be taxed as ordinary income. In my experience, clients who come to Cardinal for retirement planning are keenly interested in talking about how their IRA or 401(k) is invested and whether or not they are growing. That's because the average client has a large amount of financial assets held in IRAs and other types of qualified plans. This chapter will fully cover the details of

Gerald R. Ford.

IRAs, including distribution plans, beneficiaries, transfers and rollovers, and Roth conversions. The next chapter will cover other types of investments.

ORIGIN OF THE IRA
(INDIVIDUAL RETIREMENT ARRANGEMENT)

Gerald R. Ford signed into law the Employee Retirement Income Security Act (ERISA) on September 2, 1974. Here's how he explained the importance of the law that created what we know as IRAs, which have become a foundation of our national retirement system:

> Dramatic growth in recent years has thrust private pension plans into a central role in determining how older Americans live in their retirement years....Growth in pension plans has brought with it a host of new problems. Many workers have ultimately lost their benefits—even after relatively long service—because when they left jobs, they thereby gave up rights to hard-earned pension benefits. Others have sustained hardships because their companies folded with insufficient funds in the pension plan to pay promised pensions. In addition, some pension funds have been invested primarily for the benefit of the companies or plan administrators, not for the workers. It is essential to bring some order and humanity into this welter of different and sometimes inequitable retirement plans within private industry. Today, with great pleasure, I am signing into law a landmark measure that may finally give the American worker solid protection in his pension plan. Under this law, which is entitled the Employee Retirement Income Security Act of 1974, the men and women of our labor force will have much more clearly defined rights to pension funds and greater assurances that retirement dollars will be there when they are needed. Employees will also be given greater tax incentives to provide for their own retirement if a company plan is unavailable. It is certainly appropriate that this law be signed on Labor Day, since this Act makes a brighter future for almost all the men and women of our labor force.

To put IRAs in perspective:

- Americans hold $24.2 trillion in retirement assets. By comparison, the entire national debt in 2014 was $18.1 trillion.
- $7.3 trillion is held in IRAs; $6.6 trillion is held in 401(k)s, 403(b)s, 457(b)s, and other defined contribution plans.
- Americans rolled over $324 billion from plans to IRAs in 2013.

Your IRA may be one of your largest financial assets and you may be counting on it for your retirement income. The biggest mistakes in handling these assets usually are not about how your IRA is invested; rather, mistakes are usually made in other areas, such as account transfers, beneficiary designations, and required minimum distributions. **If one wrong transaction is made with an IRA or other retirement plan, it might well be irreversible and cause big tax liabilities and possibly penalties. Don't try IRA planning on your own—consult with a trained and knowledgeable IRA expert.**

The three main IRA planning areas our clients need help with are rollovers and transfers, beneficiary designations, and required minimum distributions (RMDs). IRA money is referred to as "qualified," which means the taxes due on principal and earnings are deferred. (Exceptions are Roth IRAs and nondeductible IRA and 401(k) contributions, see below). Qualified money is held by a custodian who is responsible for following Internal Revenue Service (IRS) rules. In order to retain the tax-deferred status, the money must stay in the IRA and be titled in the IRA owner's name. **If the owner takes possession of the money and fails to precisely follow every step of very complex rules, the owner will be pushed into a high tax bracket, the IRA will be canceled, and the taxes on the IRA will all come due in one year. A very high income resulting from a full distribution creates a host of other problems as well.**

Ed Slott has developed a well-deserved reputation as "America's IRA expert." In addition to publishing books and educating consumers through Public Television specials, Ed's company provides extensive training about the complexities of IRAs to financial advisors nationwide. I went into Ed's Elite Advisor training thinking I already knew most of what he was going to teach me. Was I wrong! The premise of the Elite Advisors is that most professionals don't have the specific training needed to help clients get the most of their IRAs. The training highlights case after case in which the advisor or attorney messed up through ignorance of the law and IRS rules. At Cardinal, when we prepare financial

SUMMARY: IRA STRATEGIZING

- Ed Slott, a CPA, has developed a reputation as "America's IRA expert" (see IRAHELP.com). I have completed IRA-specific training with Ed beyond my Certified Financial Planner™ training, and we continually receive training in IRA planning. Don't try IRA planning on your own. Seek an advisor and attorney who know what they're doing with IRAs.

- Transfer IRA money from custodian to custodian. Don't touch the money unless you want to risk paying taxes on it.

- Update your beneficiary forms regularly. IRA money goes straight to the named beneficiary after death, bypassing the will.

- Required minimum distributions (RMD) must start after age 70½. In simple terms, you are now old, you have avoided taxes for years, and the government wants its money. Mistakes are costly and it is very hard to plead for mercy from the IRS.

- Stockpiling money in an IRA and taking only the minimum distributions so you can leave it to your kids is not a smart estate planning strategy. There are ways to pay the taxes during your lifetime and leave tax-free money to your heirs.

- Long-term care implications for IRAs: This is the second place your caretakers usually go for money to pay the long-term care bill (after your Social Security check). IRA withdrawals are taxable as ordinary income, and the long-term care bill creates a corresponding tax deduction as a medical expense. But you need smart planning to optimize using your IRA for long-term care.

plans we consult with Ed's team of technical experts to make sure we are advising clients correctly. As just noted, mistakes can be costly and the IRS allows little or no leeway. I have great confidence in our work knowing that Ed and his team are at my disposal when solving problems for my clients. **It bears repeating: Don't try IRA planning and management at home—seek professional advice from an IRA trained expert.**

The Nuts and Bolts of IRAs

I'll explain the nuts and bolts of how IRAs work, and illustrate with a number of real stories the kinds of expensive problems that result from carelessness or a lack of understanding of complex IRS rules.

Rollovers and Transfers

A rollover or transfer of an IRA is when it is moved to a new account at a different custodian. This is a transaction that's very easy to mess up and cause income taxation on the whole balance. Don't take possession of the money! Make sure the money transfers custodian to custodian and you don't touch it. You might hear about the 60-day rule, but I suggest ignoring it. If you want or need some of the money, the new custodian can distribute only the amount you need after the whole of the IRA is protected from income tax. Give us a call at Cardinal (or find us on the web at PlanWithCardinal.com); or you can find another Ed Slott Elite Advisor at IRAhelp.com.

Marshall and Elizabeth (whom we met in chapter 4) had just rolled over $180,000 of their IRAs into an annuity/life hybrid policy that paid long-term care insurance for life, and set up minimum distributions to happen automatically for as long as they live. Marshall especially liked not having to worry about arranging for minimum distributions every year. He told me he did not anticipate ever needing his IRAs and wanted to leave any principal remaining to his three sons after Elizabeth and he were gone. Marshall also had a secret IRA that he was using to support Christian Missions of the World via his distributions. On Marshall's recommendation, I studied Ed Slott's books and quickly came up with an additional plan to sell them two more policies. The first used the remaining $300,000 of his IRAs to buy an annuity guaranteeing Marshall and Elizabeth $18,000 per year as long as either of them is alive. The annual payments mean that minimum distributions are set for life for both of them. The second policy, a survivorship life insurance policy owned by their son who lives closest to them, will pay $300,000 to all three sons tax free when the second of Marshall and Elizabeth dies. The annual premium for this policy is $10,000, and it is being paid by the remaining after-tax portion of the $18,000 annuity payment. See what a savvy knowledge of investment and insurance products can accomplish?

Only a month after I delivered these policies, I learned that Marshall had passed away suddenly. Based on what Marshall had told me about his secret IRA, I helped his son direct the entire balance to the charity he was supporting. Even though I didn't know Marshall long, we hit it off really well. I am very grateful to him for introducing me to the work of Ed Slott. As it turned out, Marshall was mentoring me while paying me to plan his estate.

In Rebecca's case, an employer not well versed in the rules made a mistake that cost her a lot of money. Rebecca retired early in 2012 and relied on her employer for advice about her qualified money. The employer told her the $90,000 in her 401(k) could be rolled over to an IRA, so she rolled it over through her local bank. Her pension plan had a cash-out option of $150,000 and the employer told Rebecca the check had to be made out to her to relieve the employer of the liability. Rebecca went ahead and took the check. The employer withheld 20% federal tax and 7% state tax, leaving Rebecca with $110,000. The IRS got $10,000 more when she filed her taxes, netting her about $100,000. Feeling flush—with money she never should have been given—she bought a $25,000 car she didn't need and over the past two years has spent $25,000 more. She now has $50,000 left of what was a $150,000 IRA. Because Medicare uses 2012 income to calculate 2015 higher-income surcharges (a stealth tax) for Part B and Part D premiums, Rebecca was assessed an additional $200 monthly for her 2015 Medicare (see appendix D). My firm appealed to Medicare on her behalf about the surcharges and got them refunded. I wish we could do the same for the missing $100,000 of her IRA money. To satisfy the employer's need to make the check out to Rebecca, we could have requested instead that it be made out to a bank for the benefit of (FBO) Rebecca for $151,000. It's a simple solution, and we do this all the time for clients when handling rollovers and transfers.

Kevin and Vanessa are a couple whose somewhat unconventional relationship is a good example of the complicated real-world scenarios we encounter all the time. Kevin had been married twice before and Vanessa once. They met when they both worked for a large power company. While they are not married to each other, they have a long-term relationship and intend to stay together for the rest of their lives. When Kevin retired at age 65, he no longer had money in 401(k) accounts because they were given to two ex-wives. Lucky for him, he had a pension plan offering him either $2,800 per month for life or a cash-out option of $405,000. But the cash-out was risky because if he died before age 65, no one in his family would receive the $405,000, and Vanessa couldn't get it because they're not married. I helped Kevin roll the $405,000 into an IRA, custodian to custodian, so no taxes are currently due. We split the money up into four buckets of $100,000 each. The first $100,000 went into an immediate annuity that pays Kevin $870 per month for ten years until he is 75. The second $100,000 is in a deferred annuity with guaranteed growth and guaranteed income available to Kevin anytime he wants it. The third $100,000 is in an FDIC-insured interest-paying CD (certificate of deposit) linked to a basket of stocks that matures in five years. The fourth $100,000 is in a managed account split between stocks and bonds. Vanessa is the beneficiary on one of Kevin's accounts. Taking these buckets together, we've spread out Kevin's financial risk, provided for some growth in his assets, given him a monthly income in retirement, and provided for his life partner.

Vanessa became sick with cancer soon after I met her and had to retire before she turned 65. Vanessa decided she didn't need any income beyond her Social Security. She was interested in growing her retirement money, postponing income taxes, and providing long-term care benefits with her retirement savings. Vanessa had $170,000 in her 401(k) and another $100,000 in what she thought was a 401(k) from a former employer. She thought it was earning 6% so she let it sit there. When we got on the phone with the plan administrator, we learned this was actually a pension plan with a cash-out option having no survivor benefits. Had Vanessa died from the cancer, this $100,000 would have been lost. We immediately cashed it out and rolled it into her IRA. Vanessa currently has $200,000 of her IRA in annuities guaranteed and growing, and $75,000 of her IRA in a managed account of short-duration bonds. The whole $275,000 is protected from income tax until she is 70½. When and if she needs long-term care, the annuity portion of Vanessa's savings has an enhanced long-term care benefit. We were able to provide some long-term care benefits from an insurance company for an otherwise uninsurable client. This made Vanessa very happy.

Minimum Distributions

Minimum distributions from an IRA can be a confusing subject. **You must take your first Required Minimum Distribution for the year in which you turn age 70½.** However, the first payment can be delayed until April 1 of the following year. For all subsequent years, you must take the RMD by December 31 of the current year. Retirement plan participants and IRA owners are responsible for taking the correct amount of RMDs from their accounts on time every year, and they face stiff penalties for failure to take them.

A big misconception is that it is somehow wrong to take out some of your balance before you turn 70½. But depending on your tax situation and your need or desire for the income, starting sooner might make sense, as long as you are over 59½. Another big misconception is that one should only take the minimum after age 70. Withdrawing more than the minimum distribution, and paying the tax slowly, may make more sense in the long run and be better for your heirs.

If the IRA is the inheritance you are planning to leave the kids, consider purchasing some life insurance that will come to them tax free—you can use the minimum distributions to pay the premiums. There are a lot of options, so it's worthwhile to consult a professional who is trained in IRAs.

If you have more than one IRA, the required minimum distribution is calculated by adding up the balances in all your IRAs as of December 31 of the previous year. The total distribution for the current year can be taken from just one of the multiple IRAs. It can be taken anytime during the year. This calculation becomes harder as you age, and mistakes are costly. Consider combining your IRAs and creating a distribution plan that will last a lifetime. A trained IRA advisor can show you how to do that.

Victor's story highlights several important aspects of IRA planning. Victor passed away in 1995 at age 68 and left his IRA to his wife, Edith. Because Edith was a spouse beneficiary, she was able to retitle Victor's IRA into her own name. This further delayed the start of minimum distributions because she was younger than Victor. Edith also had her own IRA. Edith changed the beneficiaries on both IRAs to her two children right after Victor passed; Sybil was 36 and Jackson was 30 at the time. In 2003, Edith began taking required minimum distributions from both of her IRAs and continued RMDs until her death in 2012. Jackson and Sybil, as beneficiaries, split the two IRAs in half, creating inherited IRAs from Edith. Both Sybil and Jackson started RMDs in 2013, at different amounts because Sybil was 54 and Jackson was 48. Minimum distributions on inherited IRAs must be calculated using IRS tables of life expectancy over the life of the beneficiary; life expectancy cannot be recalculated each year on an inherited IRA. An inherited asset like this is known as the "Stretch IRA."

In 2014, Jackson decided to open a business with the nonqualified cash portion of his inheritance. He went through the $400,000 he inherited in cash pretty quickly. As with most new small businesses, the launch required much more money than he had thought. In January 2015, Jackson emptied both of his inherited IRAs to fund the business. He netted another $400,000 of the $550,000 IRA balance after tax withholding. His net taxes when he files for 2015 will exceed the withholding because a distribution of $550,000 in one year pushed him into a very high tax bracket. Hopefully he has a good tax advisor who can write off some of the business losses, because he does not have the money to pay the additional tax. **The lesson from Jackson's part of the story is to involve your adult children in your IRA planning and make your IRA advisors available to them before and after you pass away.** In this particular situation, an IRA beneficiary trust might have been a good option to prevent Jackson's tax liability. But stretch IRAs are complicated, and you need to set up this type of account correctly to ensure that the trust is eligible to carry out the stretch IRA for your kids into retirement.

Sybil is in the fortunate position of having $570,000 in inherited IRAs and $600,000 in her own IRA. She is 56 now and plans to retire at 66. In her financial plan, we showed Sybil how the distributions on the inherited IRA will play out for her between now and age 84 when, under the standard government distribution plan, her inherited IRA would be empty. Concerned about the possibility of a market correction or two like the one that occurred in 2008, Sybil decided to shop for an annuity that would offer guaranteed payouts larger than the uncertain payouts in her investment account, and also guarantee those larger payments for the rest of her life. She decided to transfer her own $600,000 IRA to a fee-based account that will be managed to grow, and to start receiving income at age 66 and possibly delayed to age 70½ (which would allow the principal to continue growing). We also wrote Sybil a $500,000 life insurance policy with a $6,300 annual premium that names her two children as beneficiaries. If she pays the premium as long as she lives (or up to age 100), the policy will pay $500,000 tax free to her beneficiaries. If Sybil needs money for long-term care during her lifetime, she can draw upon the $500,000 life insurance tax free.

The story of Victor and his family is probably different from your own story, and your financial planning needs may be different from theirs. But this example shows you how complicated IRA planning can be, and underscores the importance of planning in partnership with trained and experienced advisors.

Beneficiaries

It seems like it should be a simple thing to make sure that the beneficiaries you choose to inherit your assets get the money. But because multiple documents are often involved, this can trip people up. In 2009, the U.S. Supreme Court unanimously ruled that an ex-spouse was entitled to receive retirement plan money because she was named on the beneficiary form, even though she had waived her rights to that money in a divorce decree (*Kennedy v. Plan Administrator for Dupont Savings and Investment Plan,* No. 07-636, decided January 26, 2009). As a result, Kari Kennedy lost a $402,000 inheritance, even though her father intended her to be the beneficiary and thought he had made that desire official. In my training with Ed Slott we studied case after case demonstrating that the money goes to the person named on the beneficiary form. Beneficiary designations trump the will, trump divorce decrees, and trump remarriages.

Beneficiaries need to be updated after births, deaths, marriages, divorces, remarriage, illness, job change, a child reaching age 21, an inheritance received, gifts made, the purchase or sale of a home...any conceivable change in personal or family circumstances that affects the status of one's assets. When we prepare financial plans, we discover that many clients hadn't even thought about updating beneficiaries since they originally enrolled in their plan. Most of them think the will, divorce decree, marriage license, etc., takes care of this for them, but that's incorrect. **Your beneficiary designation is for your family; get it right.** Most clients name their current spouse as primary beneficiary and their children as contingent beneficiaries. A surviving spouse can delay distributions until 70½ and recalculate life expectancy after that. If there is no spouse, the children are usually the beneficiaries. But you can choose to name anyone as beneficiary to your IRA. Any living beneficiary who is a real person can spread distributions over their lifetime, further deferring taxes. When a client passes away, the heirs are often shocked to learn that beneficiary designations trump the will.

THE VALUE OF AN INDEPENDENT FINANCIAL PLANNER

Robert and Sarah (whom you met in chapter 2) had started moving all of their remaining financial assets under the management of a large national investment advisory firm. Robert had responded to an advertising pitch highlighting their dislike of annuities. He told this firm that he and Sarah needed $80,000 per year before taxes to live on. The firm's recommendation was to invest all of their money in blue chip stocks. Before we gave our opinion, we created a cash flow projection for Robert and Sarah for the next five years. We showed them that Social Security, existing annuity income, and Robert's pension will create more income than $80,000 without touching their investments until his IRA requires it.

We did a risk tolerance exercise with Sarah and Robert that showed us that their investment preferences are more conservative than when Robert had consulted with the large national firm. Since he was only two years away from having to take required minimum distributions at age 70½, we invested his IRA in a moderate growth portfolio. Sarah was nine years away from 70½, so we invested her IRA in a growth portfolio.

As soon as the custodian receives proof of death, they get in touch with the named beneficiary and offer them a check, a transfer, or a retitling of the existing account. By the time a will goes to probate, the IRA has already been distributed. A good advisor communicates with you regularly and will stay on top of this situation for you.

Roth IRAs

Roth IRAs differ from traditional IRAs in that they are tax free instead of tax deferred. Sounds pretty good, doesn't it? The money going into a Roth IRA is already taxed up front, where the traditional IRA is pre-tax money. Roth IRAs also have no required minimum distributions. **You can convert your traditional IRA into a Roth IRA by simply paying the income taxes**. But that means you need to have enough cash sitting on the sidelines to pay the income taxes, or a Roth conversion does not make much sense. We can space the conversion out in pieces over several years if that works best for you. I suggest that you gift some money to your kids and grandkids to set up their own Roth IRAs, and encourage them to contribute as well.

Learn from the Mistakes of Others

A technical expert from Ed Slott's company wrote an article about private letter rulings that I have paraphrased below.

> Learn from the mistakes of others. You can't live long enough to make them all yourself.
>
> —Eleanor Roosevelt

We like to paraphrase this quote. Learn from the mistakes of others—it's cheaper that way. Here's what I mean. During one week in 2015, the IRS issued five private letter rulings (PLRs) dealing with IRAs. PLRs don't have the force of precedent—they only apply in the specific, individual case—but they strongly suggest how the IRS views a given situation and how it is likely to rule in a similar case. Don't let these problems happen to you or to your clients.

The first one dealt with the distribution of plan assets from a bankrupt company. The employee provided information for a direct transfer of the plan assets to another plan. The custodian could not reach any of the contacts listed, so they issued a check to the plan participant—minus the 20% mandatory tax withholding. The participant did not receive the check. He did not discover anything was wrong until he received IRS Form 1099-R for the distribution. **The moral of the story: Always, Always, ALWAYS follow up on your transfers**. This man's failure to follow up caused the loss of 20% of his retirement account (i.e., the amount of income tax that was sent to IRS). He will get back any overpayment of taxes when he files his tax return, but he cannot put the funds back in his plan (he did not ask IRS to allow him to do this).

Another PLR dealt with a very common problem. The wrong box got checked. The IRA funds went into a nonqualified account. This was a direct transfer. The account owner did not get a 1099-R for the distribution. But he got a love letter from the IRS asking for taxes on the amount of the distribution. **The moral of the story, again: Always, Always, ALWAYS follow up on your transfers**. Also make sure you follow up on rollovers. This mistake happens all too frequently with rollovers as well.

The next PLR involved another direct transfer for a new investment. **The account owner thought the new custodian could hold IRA funds**. Custodian 1 did not follow its own internal procedures and Custodian 2 was not an IRA custodian. No 1099-R was issued since this was a "direct transfer." The account owner discovered the problem when he inquired about his required distribution for the year.

Another PLR was also for a new investment. The account owner was assured that the new investment could be made with IRA funds. This one was done as a 60-day rollover, so the 1099-R did not alarm the account owner. Her clue came when she got a K-1 from the new investment that did not indicate that her shares were being held in the name of her IRA. **The moral of the story for these two mistakes: Ask for a beneficiary form. If you are opening a new IRA investment, you should have an IRA agreement AND a beneficiary form. If the custodian can't give you a beneficiary form, then you do not have an IRA account. It's as simple as that.**

This last example is a common required minimum distribution (RMD) error. The individual had three retirement accounts—an employer plan, a SEP IRA (Simplified Employee Pension; it is designed for small employers and uses an IRA as the receptacle for the money), and a traditional IRA. **His tax advisor told him to calculate the RMDs separately and that he could then take the balance from any one of his accounts.** He elected to take the distribution from his SEP IRA. **The problem: You cannot take an RMD for one type of account from a different type of account.** Your IRA distribution cannot come from an employer plan and vice versa (SEP and SIMPLE accounts are considered IRA accounts for RMD purposes). Therefore, he had not taken an RMD from his employer plan for the year. **Unfortunately, the lesson here is that even a trusted advisor may not know all the RMD rules.**

These mistakes cost the account owners anywhere from $3,000 to $10,000 *in IRS fees alone* for filing a PLR request, not to mention the substantial income lost as a result of the errors. They also had to pay a professional to prepare the PLR request. Hopefully you can learn from these mistakes of others and avoid them—it's cheaper that way. And Cardinal stands ready to guide you through the thickets of IRA and IRS rules and regulations.

SUMMARY: IRA STRATEGIZING

- Ed Slott, a CPA, has developed a reputation as "America's IRA expert" (see IRAHELP.com). I have completed IRA-specific training with Ed beyond my Certified Financial Planner™ training, and we continually receive training in IRA planning. Don't try IRA planning on your own. Seek an advisor and attorney who know what they're doing with IRAs.

- Transfer IRA money from custodian to custodian. Don't touch the money unless you want to risk paying taxes on it.

- Update your beneficiary forms regularly. IRA money goes straight to the named beneficiary after death, bypassing the will.

- Required minimum distributions (RMD) must start after age 70½. In simple terms, you are now old, you have avoided taxes for years, and the government wants its money. Mistakes are costly and it is very hard to plead for mercy from the IRS.

- Stockpiling money in an IRA and taking only the minimum distributions so you can leave it to your kids is not a smart estate planning strategy. There are ways to pay the taxes during your lifetime and leave tax-free money to your heirs.

- Long-term care implications for IRAs: This is the second place your caretakers usually go for money to pay the long-term care bill (after your Social Security check). IRA withdrawals are taxable as ordinary income, and the long-term care bill creates a corresponding tax deduction as a medical expense. But you need smart planning to optimize using your IRA for long-term care.

CHAPTER 6 | **INVESTING YOUR MONEY AND LIVING ON IT FOR THE REST OF YOUR LIFE**

"I violated the Noah rule: Predicting rain doesn't count; building arks does."
—Warren Buffett

I once worked with Jared, who invested 100% of his 401(k) in the stock of the company we worked for. The stock was riding high for a while and then whammy, the company couldn't swallow a large acquisition, filed for bankruptcy, and down the drain went Jared's 25 years of hard work and several hundred thousand dollars. That's a hard way to learn the principle of diversification. Don't put all your eggs in one basket, or even two or three baskets. When investing in stocks, you should have holdings in several companies spread across several industries and even several countries. That way, if one company goes bankrupt, or otherwise takes a big financial hit, you can make it up with gains from the others. A mutual fund or a professionally managed portfolio of stocks and bonds makes investments for you in a large number of companies. This is called diversification, and this is the cardinal investing principle we follow at Cardinal.

Types of Risk

Managing risk is the key to a successful investment strategy. You need to understand the different types of risk, as well as your own tolerance levels for them in the context of your overall financial plan.

SUMMARY: STRATEGIZING INVESTMENT RISK

- Stop chasing return and start managing risk.

- As you age, income becomes more important than account balances.

- Consider fixed indexed annuities, which can provide lifetime income and some nice guarantees.

- Long-term care implications of your investments: Using long-term care services, paid for by you, will create a big dent in your savings and income. Many fixed indexed annuities have long-term care enhancements and don't require you to answer health history questions. The need for long-term care funds could come at the wrong time relative to the ebb and flow of markets, so buying these enhancements could be a good choice.

Market risk is what most people think of when they hear the word "risk." When investors are scared, when banks are afraid to lend, or when consumers stop spending, the value of your stocks decreases. Those potential losses represent the market risk for everyone who owns stocks. The ways to mitigate stock market risk are to invest part of your money in products that stay even or go up in value when stock prices go down, for example, cash, selling stock short, and put options.

Interest rate risk means you might lose money on your investment when interest rates go up. Rising interest rates are generally bad for both stocks and bonds.

Inflation or purchasing power risk is the risk that your money will be worth less to you in the future; in other words, a given amount of money will buy fewer goods and services in the future. This is the risk of avoiding other risks by being too conservative in your investing. The strategy for mitigating inflation risk is to own a variety of asset types, including stocks, real estate, and gold.

Liquidity risk is the risk that you can't turn your money into cash quickly if you need it quickly. Liquidity risk is mitigated by holding some cash plus stocks and bonds.

Credit risk is the possibility that you own stock in a company that will be unable to pay its bills or have to go out of business. Again, the way to mitigate credit risk is to have a diversified asset portfolio.

It's a risky world out there. It is impossible to avoid all types of risk unless you don't have any money. As I've advised throughout this book, get professional help when investing your money. The chart below provides a simple way to understand the risks associated with the various kinds of investments that tend to appeal to the seniors who come to Cardinal for help

Managing Risk: Green Money, Red Money, and Yellow Money

A simple way to think about the risks you are taking with your money is to divide the pot into "green money" and "red money." (Thanks to Gradient Financial Group for this concept.) Green money is "know so" and red money is "hope so." In other words, green is money you know you are going to receive; red is money you hope will produce a good return, but you don't know for sure. Examples of green money include bank CDs, your Social Security check, a company pension, fixed annuities, and government bonds. Examples of red money are stocks, corporate bonds, options, mutual funds, alternatives (such as gold, silver, and other commodities), and ETFs (Exchange Traded Funds, similar to a mutual fund). The money you need to live on

Investment Vehicle	Market Risk	Inflation Risk	Interest Rate Risk	Liquidity Risk	Credit Risk
Equities/Stock	High	Low	Moderate	Low	Moderate
Bonds	Low	High	High	Low	Moderate
Equity-Indexed Annuities	Low	Moderate	Low	High	Low
Fixed-Rate Annuities	None	High	Low	High	Low
Bank CDs	None	High	Low	High	None
Cash/Money Market	None	High	None	None	Low
Real Estate	Moderate	Low	Low	High	None
Gold/ Commodities	High	Opposite	Moderate	Low	Low
Options	High	None	Opposite	High	Moderate

should be parked in green money. The money you don't need or want for a while, and which you can afford to lose, can be invested in red money. Red money becomes yellow money when you place it in the hands of a professional money manager. Your money is still at risk when it is yellow, but the risk is calculated, diversified, and managed. Professional, fee-based management is now available if you have as little as $50,000 to invest.

When we work with new clients, we help them learn about their personal tolerance for market risk. How much market risk can you afford to take? How much do you desire to take? What effect will it have upon you, emotionally and financially, to suddenly lose part of your money? We quantify your risk and then match it against your current investments.

Sybil, whom you met in chapter 5, hired us to prepare a financial plan for her. Three years ago she inherited a good sum of money and now she is planning for retirement. We plugged all of her current investments into a calculator provided by Morningstar. Morningstar provided us with a page of analysis on every position in her portfolio. The report quantifies the risk Sybil is taking with every stock she owns and shows how well the stock is performing given the associated market risk. Morningstar also tallied up the fees Sybil is being charged. (A copy of the summary page of this Morningstar report is in appendix E.) We compared Sybil's Morningstar analysis to her risk profile and looked for gaps between where she thought she was and where she wants to be. We also looked at inflation risk, liquidity risk, and credit risk. We then suggested changes she can make in her investments to line up her portfolio with her desired risk. As a result, Sybil moved her inherited IRA into an equity-indexed annuity with an income rider (see the sidebar on page 55), her personal IRA into a professionally managed portfolio of large-dividend-paying stocks, her mother's trust to a local bank, and her personal nonqualified money to a credit union.

———◆———

Ross and Fiona are a couple I met when they attended a financial planning workshop I led at their church. Ross retired in 2012 at age 62; Fiona continues to work, has a small employee retirement plan, and will receive a pension when she retires. Ross receives a pension of $1,100 monthly, and if he predeceases Fiona she will receive the same amount for the rest of her life. Ross managed his 401(k) himself through the years, getting his counsel from his buddies at work, research on the Internet, and the goal maker program within his 401(k). At its highest point his 401(k) balance was over $400,000. But the stock market crash of 2008 was more than he could stomach as he looked ahead to retirement a few years later. So he

FIXED INDEXED ANNUITIES

Fixed indexed annuities with income riders are a poorly understood and much criticized insurance policy. Like any investment, if it is purchased by the wrong client for the wrong reasons in the wrong amount, it is a bad deal. But a fixed indexed annuity can also be a useful and valuable policy for some people.

The biggest gripe about fixed indexed annuities is that your money is tied up for several years. The second honk is that the costs and fees are high and mostly hidden from the untrained eye. A good amount of those fees and costs pay the insurance company for the guarantees you are buying. They guarantee that you will never lose your principal, yet they share a portion of your upside gains in the market. Through an income rider, which you pay for, the insurance company guarantees you an annual or monthly payment that will last as long as you or your spouse live. And the payments continue even if the principal is depleted. The longer you wait to begin taking payments, the larger the payment. Many companies selling these policies offer a long-term care enhancement benefit that doubles or triples the income rider amount for a period of time if you need such care.

If you purchase a fixed indexed annuity with part of your retirement money, you will tie up that money for a long time and you will pay fees within the contract. What you will receive in return is protection from an insurance company against some very scary things: market losses, outliving your savings, and not having enough money to pay long-term care expenses. An experienced financial advisor can help you figure out whether or not this is a good choice for you.

converted his 401(k) to all cash in early 2009. Consequently, Ross missed the bull market that started in 2009 and has continued for the past several years.

Ross and Fiona came in to see us in late 2014, when his 401(k) had decreased to $221,000. He had made several withdrawals to supplement his reduced Social Security and pension (reduced because he retired early). Now 64 and retired, Ross needed to make this $221,000 last for the rest of his and Fiona's lives. He did not want to take the risk of getting back into the stock market. We split the funds into two buckets:

REVERSE MORTGAGES: BEWARE

$ A reverse mortgage is designed for people age 62 or older who are cash poor and home equity rich. It allows an older homeowner to spend the equity in his or her home without having to make any mortgage payments until they die or move out of the home. I generally don't recommend a reverse mortgage unless the income is very much needed for your health and welfare and you have no other alternative sources of money. The home will be sold after you pass away or move out, and the loan balance will have to be paid off from the proceeds. Your heirs will only receive what's left, if anything. I don't have a client story because I have never had a client implement a reverse mortgage. But there are lots of commercials on TV aired by banks offering reverse mortgages and pitched by celebrities. Proceed with caution and ask an advisor who has no stake in the deal for an opinion before you do anything.

$75,000 for current income and $150,000 in an account he is not going to touch for seven years. The $75,000 is now in a laddered bond fund (a series of bonds that mature at different times) that pays him $15,000 per year for between five and six years. Fiona has about $40,000 in her 401(k) and is still working and contributing. We will use her money to get them through years six and seven. The $150,000 is guaranteed by an insurance company to grow in the next seven years to the point where they can pay Ross and Fiona $15,000 annually as long as either one of them is alive.

The lesson here is that trying to time the market without professional help can put you in a bad situation. The closer you are to retirement, or if you're already retired, the less risk you need to take.

You met Nicole in chapter 4; she came to Cardinal for help with Medicare planning, and then we looked at her assets to plan for the eventuality of long-term care. After we constructed Nicole's financial plan, she elected to invest her nonqualified portfolio of $521,000 in a managed portfolio of high-quality dividend-paying stocks. This investment reduced her market risk but still left her with more risk than she wanted to hold. Recently, she came to us needing to increase her income by $3,000 per month. Our recommended solution was to move $300,000 of her $521,000 into an equity-indexed annuity with an income rider. She plans to leave the $300,000 annuity alone for ten years and allow it to grow, tax deferred. The insurance company guarantees her an income starting in ten years at a minimum of $36,000 annually. The remaining value of the dividend-paying stocks will start at $221,000 and we will draw that account down at the rate of $3,000 per month as long as she needs that amount.

She is able to take out a good portion of the $3,000 per month tax free because it is simply returning her principal. Nicole will have a gap in her income in her early 70s when the account is depleted. We will fill that gap for her out of other investments, or simply start taking money from the annuity earlier than originally intended and at a smaller amount. Nicole has substantially reduced her market risk, increased her inflation risk, and begun using liquidity to create income.

One principle of financial planning for retirement stands out to me as very important yet little understood: **When you get to be 65, and then 75 and you're looking forward, income and the guarantees of income should become much more important to you than returns on investment.** Cardinal can help you figure out how to create a diversified asset portfolio that takes this recommended shift in perspective into account as you get older.

SUMMARY: STRATEGIZING INVESTMENT RISK

- Stop chasing return and start managing risk.

- As you age, income becomes more important than account balances.

- Consider fixed indexed annuities, which can provide lifetime income and some nice guarantees.

- Long-term care implications of your investments: Using long-term care services, paid for by you, will create a big dent in your savings and income. Many fixed indexed annuities have long-term care enhancements and don't require you to answer health history questions. The need for long-term care funds could come at the wrong time relative to the ebb and flow of markets, so buying these enhancements could be a good choice.

CHAPTER 7 | LIFE INSURANCE, ESTATE PLANNING, AND YOUR LEGACY

T his chapter focuses on life insurance. The stories I'll share about the experiences of a few of my clients will demonstrate how life insurance relates to other assets like IRAs and fits into the overall picture of strategic and effective estate planning. They will also highlight some of the complications to watch out for and problems that can be avoided with good planning.

Maybe the name Kenneth Feinberg is familiar to you. He was appointed by President Bush to determine compensation for victims of the September 11 terrorist attacks and their families, and later by President Obama to do the same for the families harmed by the BP Deepwater Horizon oil well blowout in the Gulf of Mexico. Feinberg wrote a column for the *New York Times* explaining how working with the September 11 families changed his own outlook on estate planning. It is worth quoting at length, because what he learned highlights both the importance of good planning and the shocking lack of such planning among so many Americans.

> In the last 30 years, presidents, governors, mayors and others have delegated to me the unenviable task of putting a value to the lives of people who are already dead....
>
> In taking on these tasks, I have come to realize that, whatever your personal wealth, money is a poor substitute for loss. It neither tempers the grief accompanying traumatic death or physical injury nor fills the void left after tragic loss of life. During my administration of the September 11th Victim Compensation Fund, I recall one mother responding to the $3 million she would receive for the death of her son. "I have a better idea," she said. "Keep the money and bring my son back."

I have also become much more fatalistic, which has influenced my own personal financial planning. In effect, I've received on-the-job training for managing my own wealth and protecting it for my wife and family. After the 2001 attacks, I sought the advice of a financial planner having witnessed firsthand what can happen when people don't have expert financial advice.

The 9/11 fund offered free financial advice to all claimants receiving compensation. Goldman Sachs, JPMorgan Chase and others stood ready to help, but only 78 of 5,300 eligible claimants took advantage of the opportunity. "We don't need any expert advice," was the overwhelming response.

After meeting with the planner, I updated my will, something I had been putting off. Over half the victims on Sept. 11 did not have one. Given that they were relatively young and in good health with excellent jobs, they seem not to have thought it was necessary. I suddenly found it necessary. I also selected a law firm specializing in trusts and estates that knows exactly how I want my wealth distributed after my death.

It was also important to me to avoid the problems I occasionally confronted after Sept. 11, when angry siblings, parents and relatives declared war with one another over the victim's assets and argued over the 9/11 fund compensation. When millions of dollars are suddenly available for distribution, family members, fiancés and same-sex partners sometimes engage in bitter arguments. So I made sure that my wife and three children had a clear understanding of who gets what by providing each of them a detailed memorandum listing all of my assets and an explanation of how my wealth should be distributed after my death.

I also bought substantial additional life insurance. I bought a mix of term and whole life insurance, because I wanted short-term protection in the event of my untimely death and a long-term investment vehicle. I was astounded to learn that *over half the victims of the Sept. 11 attacks had no life insurance* (emphasis added). Were it not for the 9/11 fund, such a grievous oversight would have placed many victims' families at financial risk.

When it came to my investments, long-term safety and gradual growth suddenly seemed far more important than any short-term profits and quick gains. I wanted to be assured that the bulk of my wealth would be available for my wife, children and grandchildren.

Finally, in managing my individual portfolio, I have become a firm believer in the "cushion" theory of investment. I have saved more of my annual income than many people would consider to be necessary. Hundreds of Sept. 11 victims failed to set aside sufficient funds to provide for their families, believing that future earnings would be available to make up for any current shortfall. But the terrorist attacks interrupted such plans. Saving today is a hedge against unknown events tomorrow.

Nobody is immune from life's misfortunes. It need not be a terrorist attack or the acts of the gunmen at Virginia Tech; Newtown, Conn.; or Aurora, Colo. We all face uncertainty and risk. All the more reason to pause today and carefully plan for tomorrow.

— Kenneth Feinberg, "Money Admonitions from 9/11,"
New York Times, March 25, 2015

I personally had a similar experience. My sister Margot passed away suddenly from a brain aneurysm one morning in January 2011. I never got the chance to say goodbye and I miss her very much. She was an RN and a Nurse Practitioner and worked three jobs. Her husband Bill is a CPA. Despite having a father who was a 32-year insurance agent, and a brother in the life insurance business all her life, Margot passed with no life insurance. Bill told me at the funeral, "two incomes are great, one income sucks." I think about Margot and Bill every time a client procrastinates about buying life insurance. Margot was pretty hard headed and it was difficult to sell anything to her. If I could do it all over, I would let go of my excuses, dig in my heels, and sell both of them a policy. This is clearly a story of the plumber with leaky pipes in his own home.

Benjamin approached me while I was conducting a financial planning seminar at his church. He is 77 years old, and has type II diabetes and a pacemaker. Two years ago, Benjamin built a new home on one level so that he and his wife Daphne can live out the rest of their years there. Benjamin has two military pensions, but they have no survivor benefits. If he goes first, Daphne will have a hard time making the payments on the home. Benjamin told me he saves $2,000 per month (from his pensions and Social Security) so Daphne will have some money for house payments if he dies first. He had

---

SUMMARY: STRATEGIZING LIFE INSURANCE AND ESTATE PLANNING

- Calculate the amount of money your survivors need to receive quickly after you pass away. Consider purchasing life insurance. If you don't want to pay ongoing premiums, consider single-premium whole life insurance.

- Update all of your beneficiary designations. Beneficiary designations trump the will and go straight to the beneficiary.

- You need at least four legal documents prepared by an attorney knowledgeable about elder law: a will, a health-care power of attorney, a financial power of attorney, and a HIPAA release.

- $$$$$ Federal estate taxes are no longer relevant for estates under $5.43 million, or $10.86 million for couples. The step up in basis at death for capital gains taxes is the more relevant issue for middle-class taxpayers.

accumulated $25,000 and wanted my advice about investing this money. I suggested he look into life insurance and his response was that no one would write him a policy at his age and with his health conditions. But we were able to find one. We applied for a $100,000 policy with guaranteed premiums to age 100. The premium is $9,200 per year for five years and then decreases to $7,200 in the sixth year and remains there until age 100. Voilà—Benjamin no longer worries about Daphne's future if he should die first.

Benjamin then sent me to his aunt, who is the same age as he is. She has no savings and lives in low-income housing. I wrote her a $5,000 permanent life insurance policy for only $41 per month. She now feels relieved that the family won't need to pass the hat at her funeral. Even a small amount of life insurance can bring peace of mind.

Nicole, discussed in chapter 4, is another client who bought a single-premium life insurance policy. In her case, she used $300,000 she received from her mother's trust to buy a whole life policy. The death benefit is $540,000 initially and will grow as the cash value increases inside of her policy. Thus, her son Thomas is guaranteed to receive at least $540,000 tax free when Nicole passes. Most people don't purchase this kind of high-cost single-premium policy. In fact, they can be purchased for as little as one $5,000 premium that will buy almost $10,000 of life insurance, paid up for life. The health questions on these policies are very lenient because the insurance company gets your money up front. Also, a funeral home will generally accept the money from these policies as payment for a funeral. I find that insurance companies are usually better caretakers of your money than funeral homes.

Marshall and Elizabeth, other clients we've talked about previously, bought second-to-die life insurance worth $300,000 when he was 80 and she was 76. The annual premium is about $10,000 for twenty years. As I told you earlier, Marshall passed away from a heart attack just six weeks after the policy was issued. Marshall was really into planning for Elizabeth and their three sons; it was almost like he knew something was coming. The $10,000 premium is paid from the minimum distributions from Marshall's IRA. Those minimum distributions are guaranteed to last the rest of Elizabeth's life through the annuity we set up for them (see page 41). Elizabeth is now 79 and she has peace of mind knowing that each of her sons will receive a tax-free check for $100,000 very quickly after she dies, while time passes as her estate is settled. **Permanent life insurance does not cost as much as it used to, if you buy the right kind. I have delivered life insurance checks to hundreds of beneficiaries during my career and not once have I been asked any questions about the policy.** People are simply happy to receive some money from a deceased relative who loved them.

Four weeks before Marshall passed away, we had a meeting with his attorney. Marshall wanted me to advise the attorney directly about the documents I felt he and Elizabeth needed to put in place. **They each needed a will, a financial power of attorney (see appendix F), a health-care power of attorney, and a HIPAA release form** (HIPAA is the Health Insurance Portability and Accountability Act, and it protects the privacy of individually identifiable health information; see appendix G). Most of this work had been done previously, but he thought it needed updating. It didn't, because Marshall had planned well. However, Elizabeth did need to update these documents after Marshall died, and her sons will need the documents if she becomes incapacitated and can't make decisions for herself. I am continually shocked by the number of clients we see at Cardinal who haven't taken care of preparing these inexpensive and critical documents. Unless you have a large and complicated estate, you really don't need a world-class attorney for simple documents, and the service should only cost about $500 to $600.

Jason and Megan's story, involving a complicated long-term care scenario, was described earlier (see page 19). Jason has a cash-value life insurance policy with a death benefit of $100,000 that he purchased many years ago. Interest rates were 7%–8% when he bought the policy, but they have dropped below 2%, which means that his premium payments are not keeping up. The insurance company had been warning Jason and Megan about the impending lapse resulting from this decrease for years, but they never understood it. (A "lapse" in an insurance policy means the benefits are not available because the premium payments have not been made in time.) We read all the letters, contacted the insurance company with Jason on the line, and worked out a way to increase his monthly premiums and keep his insurance in force until age 90. Megan is going to need that $100,000 to live on after Jason passes on. We encounter many clients with cash-value life insurance policies that are destined to lapse if some change is not made. To avoid a problem like this, get a professional to review all of your existing life insurance policies and ask him or her to request a proposal/projection from the insurance company based upon current assumptions. In addition, be sure to check the beneficiary designation, as well as the contingent beneficiary.

The Beneficiary Designation

In chapter 6 we emphasized the importance of making sure you have designated beneficiaries of various assets correctly to reflect your wishes. As noted, these designations determine what happens regardless of what a will, a divorce decree, or other legal documents may say. This can be of particular urgency for life insurance policies, which may have been purchased years ago before your family circumstances changed. **I repeat: The beneficiary designation in most instances trumps the will and probate decisions.** Most clients don't know this simple fact. If you own life insurance, annuities, IRAs, or anything with a beneficiary designation, the money will pass directly to your named beneficiary, never passing through the lawyers or the will. **Make sure your beneficiary forms are up to date!** We find clients coming in the door with ex-spouses, deceased relatives, and estranged family members named as beneficiaries, their policies not having been updated for years. You don't want to make that mistake.

A recent court case underscores the risk of inattention to these details. In *Herring v. Campbell* (No. 11-40953, decided August 7, 2012), John Wayne Hunter, a retiree of Marathon Oil who participated in the company's pension plan, died without designating a beneficiary for his plan proceeds after the death of his wife the year before. His two stepsons, whom he had helped raise with his wife but never legally adopted, filed suit after Hunter's death to challenge the distribution of his retirement benefits. The company plan administrator had rejected the possibility that the stepsons might be defined as Hunter's "children" and therefore entitled to his benefits. But they cited their close relationship with Hunter, the fact that Hunter left his estate to them, and the fact that he had referred to them as his "beloved sons" in his will. However, both a lower court and the U.S. Court of Appeals agreed that, because the company's retirement plan gives the administrator discretionary authority to determine eligibility for benefits, the fact that no beneficiaries were designated negated the language in the will

"I love you wills" work great for married couples who both have been married only one time and only have children together. In such a case, the chain of inheritance is clear: "I leave everything to my wife/husband and if he/she predeceases me, everything goes to my children equally." If either of you has been married before and has children from a prior marriage, estate planning gets more complicated. For example, the union between Joe and Anita is the second marriage for each of them. Both have children from their previous marriages. When I asked them which kids get which assets, they assured me that the distribution was all taken care of in their will. Most of their assets are in IRAs that name each other as beneficiaries, and their real estate and business are held jointly. When one dies first, the other gets everything. But when the second one dies, which kids get what? Remember, what the will says doesn't count compared with the specific beneficiary designations of the IRAs, life insurance policies, and other assets with beneficiaries. **Married couples who leave it all to each other need to consider the ultimate beneficiaries after the second one dies, especially when they are in a second marriage.**

Changes in the Estate Tax

$$$$$ Wealthier citizens have recently benefited from changes to estate tax law. According to the *Wall Street Journal*, "**The federal estate tax is no longer the biggest concern for most affluent people who want to avoid taxes on wealth they leave to heirs.** For much of the past decade, it was. In 2004, for example, the estates of people who died owning assets worth more than $1.5 million—or who made gifts above that limit while alive—were subject to federal tax at top rates approaching 50%, and mar-

---

SUMMARY: STRATEGIZING LIFE INSURANCE AND ESTATE PLANNING

- Calculate the amount of money your survivors need to receive quickly after you pass away. Consider purchasing life insurance. If you don't want to pay ongoing premiums, consider single-premium whole life insurance.

- Update all of your beneficiary designations. Beneficiary designations trump the will and go straight to the beneficiary.

- You need at least four legal documents prepared by an attorney knowledgeable about elder law: a will, a health-care power of attorney, a financial power of attorney, and a HIPAA release.

- $$$$$ Federal estate taxes are no longer relevant for estates under $5.43 million, or $10.86 million for couples. The step up in basis at death for capital gains taxes is the more relevant issue for middle-class taxpayers.

---

ried couples had to set up trusts to benefit from their full $3 million estate exemption. In addition, there was extreme uncertainty as the tax bounced around from year to year and even disappeared entirely in 2010—making effective planning exceedingly difficult. Finally, in 2013, **Congress set the top estate-and-gift-tax rate at 40% and raised the exemption to $5 million per person, adjusted for inflation. [In 2016 the exemption stands at $5.45 million per person.]** Lawmakers also changed the rules so that couples don't need trusts to get their full break from Uncle Sam…. These changes have freed hundreds of thousands of affluent Americans from worrying about federal estate tax, and they may never have to…. Now many people who won't owe estate tax can reap substantial tax savings on capital gains by choosing carefully which assets to hold until death. This strategy is especially useful now that the top federal rate on long-term gains is nearly 24%, two-thirds higher than in 2012" (*Wall Street Journal*, "The New Rules of Estate Planning," October 24, 2014).

I wouldn't be surprised if you were not aware of this significant change. This again underscores the importance of working with an experienced, well-informed professional to evaluate your various assets and help you strategize all of your estate planning. In addition to the legacy of your character, the financial legacy you leave to your children and grandchildren is profoundly important to both you and them.

I am not a CPA, nor do I prepare income taxes in my financial planning practice. But I do consider myself an expert in planning how to reduce income taxes paid on retirement income. For all new clients, we review the income tax returns from the previous two years. Our affiliated CPA firm reviews the returns and advises the client through us. I don't have any good client income tax stories, but even so I encourage you to read this brief chapter as a reminder, if nothing else. And you might learn something new. The text follows the sequence of topics as presented in the book and focuses on the relevant age 65+ income tax issues about Social Security, Medicare, long-term care, IRAs, investments, life insurance, and estate planning.

Taxes on Social Security Benefits

Some people have to pay federal income taxes on their Social Security benefits. This happens only if you have other substantial income from wages, self-employment, interest, dividends, and other taxable sources that must be reported on your tax return, in addition to your benefits. "Combined income" is one-half of your Social Security benefits plus your other income. If you file a federal tax return as an "individual" and your combined income is between $25,000 and $34,000, you will pay income tax on 50% of your Social Security check. If your income is more than $34,000 you will pay taxes on up to 85% of your Social Security check, depending on your income level. If you file a joint return, the same formula holds: 50% if your income is between $32,000 and $44,000, up to 85% if your income is over $44,000. If you are married

---

SUMMARY: STRATEGIZING INCOME TAXES

- Social Security income is partially taxed.

- $$$$$ Medicare applies a surcharge to high-income beneficiaries.

- Long-term care insurance has tax benefits.

- IRAs let you postpone income taxes, but you don't avoid income taxes altogether.

- Investment income is taxed depending on how it is held.

- There are income taxes even in death.

- Long-term care implications of income taxes: Long-term care costs can be a deductible medical expense that offsets other income.

- Get professional help with your income tax preparation.

- $ The AARP will help you complete your income taxes for free if you are in need.

---

and file a separate return, you will pay income taxes on your Social Security benefits, at the same rates. All the talk you hear about "means testing" Social Security is already happening, because more affluent people are taxed on up to 85% of their benefits.

Taxes on Medicare Benefits

$$$$$ Medicare deducts income tax money from beneficiaries with higher incomes through surcharging Part B premiums and Part D premiums. Ed Slott refers to these charges as "stealth taxes," and I have to agree. For an individual, the income threshold is $85,000; for a married couple the threshold is $170,000. If you earn less than that, your Part B premium is $104.90 (in 2015) monthly and Part D costs whatever the insurance company charges you. If you exceed those income thresholds, your Part B premium can be as much as $335.70 monthly per person, and Part D can cost as much as $70.80 plus what the insurance company charges.

For 2016, Medicare uses your 2012 income tax return, so there is a lag effect. If a client has suffered a large drop in income, we help him or her appeal using the older return as a basis. The story about Rebecca in chapter 5 (see page 42) points out how difficult an appeal can be. Most of our clients have Part B and Part D charges deducted from their Social Security checks, which means that many of them with higher incomes are unaware that they are paying this stealth tax until we point it out to them. So, like Social Security, Medicare is in fact also "means tested."

Taxes on Long-Term Care Insurance

Long-term care insurance also has some income tax implications. If you itemize deductions for 2015, you can write off a certain amount of your annual premium:

Age 40 or less:	$380
Age 41–50:	$710
Age 51–60:	$1,430
Age 61–70:	$3,800
Age 71 and older:	$4,750

—Internal Revenue Code §213(d) (10)

Make sure you consult your tax advisor before taking any of these deductions.

Benefits you receive from a qualified long-term care policy are received tax free up to $330 per day in 2015. This is approximately $10,000 per month.

Taxes on IRAs

As noted in chapter 5, IRAs are an income tax postponement vehicle. Please refer to the discussion there for details. In a nutshell: Money you withdraw from your IRA (unless it is a Roth IRA) will incur income taxes and can push you into a higher tax bracket. At age 70½, the IRS requires you to start taking money out of your IRA even if you don't want or need it. If you are over 70½ and don't need to live on your minimum distribution from your IRA, consider donating your distribution through a Qualified Charitable Distribution (QCD). Talk to your tax advisor about this idea—it is a very tax-efficient way to make charitable contributions.

Taxes on Other Investments

Investment income incurs income tax in the year it is earned and received. Capital gains and dividends are currently taxed at significantly lower rates than ordinary income. Income accrued inside of annuities and life insurance policies is not taxed until it is withdrawn. If you do not itemize deductions, you are entitled to a higher standard deduction if you are age 65 or older at the end of the year. Capital assets like real estate, a business, and/or stocks and bonds receive a step up in basis at the death of the owner. Your estate must file an income tax return for the year you die.

Tax Implications of Estate Planning

Estate planning and estate settlement have many income tax implications. The first thing to know is that **life insurance proceeds are received income tax free by most beneficiaries.** Check out the 1926 income tax form in appendix H, which exempts life insurance proceeds from income tax. This is a real tax return provided to me by one of my associates at Cardinal. His great-grandfather was a bookkeeper who lived at the local YMCA. His income in 1925 was $3,147.50, and he paid income taxes amounting to $18.50. As you can see on the back page of the return, life insurance benefits were exempt from income tax; 90 years later this exemption is still intact.

Second, it's important to remember that income taxes have to be paid for the year in which a person dies. Depending on the situation, that could be complicated and/or expensive.

Third, the inherent gains in property values are stepped up in basis when a property owner dies. If a client has a farm he bought for $200,000 many years ago and he sold it for $1,000,000 today, he would owe capital gains taxes on $800,000. If the property is held until death and passed on, his heirs receive it at a basis of $1,000,000. If the heirs sold it soon after, they would probably owe no capital gains tax.

———◆———

This brief overview should suggest to you that there are simple ways to minimize the tax liabilities of your estate—if you know the mechanics of how various assets work, and the details of tax law. There can be great value to you in consulting with an expert. Cardinal Retirement Planning, like other experienced advisory firms, can provide you with these important services.

SUMMARY: STRATEGIZING INCOME TAXES

- Social Security income is partially taxed.

- $$$$$ Medicare applies a surcharge to high-income beneficiaries.

- Long-term care insurance has tax benefits.

- IRAs let you postpone income taxes, but you don't avoid income taxes altogether.

- Investment income is taxed depending on how it is held.

- There are income taxes even in death.

- Long-term care implications of income taxes: Long-term care costs can be a deductible medical expense that offsets other income.

- Get professional help with your income tax preparation.

- $ The AARP will help you complete your income taxes for free if you are in need.

CHAPTER 9

DON'T TRY THIS AT HOME:
CHOOSING YOUR ADVISORS

An attorney friend of mine enrolled in a community college course that taught him how to be his own general contractor for the construction of his new house. He told me he "could save $20,000 on the price of the new home." I suggested he just let his paralegal go and save $40,000 a year—he is much more qualified to do paralegal work in his off time than he is to build a house. You get the point! When your entire life savings, comfort, and security in retirement are on the line, you need the help of trustworthy, competent professionals.

This point was emphasized by Barbara Roper, director of investor protection at the Consumer Federation of America.

> Investors today fail basic financial literacy tests. They know nothing about how to evaluate these investments—that's why they turn to brokers and advisors for advice, and the research indicates that when they do turn to the brokers and advisors for advice, they rely extremely heavily on the recommendation, often without looking at another piece of paper, precisely because they don't feel that they have that expertise. This is a relationship that cries out for fiduciary protection because it is a relationship of trust and it's promoted as a relationship of trust. (See Kenneth Corbin, "Industry Reps Warn DoL Fiduciary Rule Will Gut Retirement Advice," www.financial-planning.com/article_listings/kenneth-corbin-845.html.)

> ## SUMMARY: CHOOSING THE RIGHT ADVISOR
>
> - Find a CFP (Certified Financial Planner™) who specializes in eldercare planning and estate planning. You can start at LetsMakeAPlan.org.
>
> - A CFP® can help you locate an elder law attorney, an estate planning attorney, and/or a CPA if needed.
>
> - Buy your insurance from an independent agent who represents several insurance companies and specializes in insurance products appropriate for seniors.
>
> - Our Cardinal principles are: Trust, Independence, Professional Designations, Verify, Fiduciary Standards, and Specialization.

If you follow my recommendations, you could need a financial advisor, an insurance agent, an accountant, and an attorney who specializes in serving retired or retiring clients. If your financial advisor is certified as a financial planner, he or she can coordinate the work of all these professionals. He or she can also refer you to other trustworthy professionals if you are unfamiliar with service providers in your area. To find a Certified Financial Planner™ in your area, go to one of these websites: LetsMakeAPlan.org or PlanWithCardinal.com.

Professional designations like CPA (Certified Public Accountant), CFP (Certified Financial Planner™), CASL (Chartered Advisor for Senior Living™), and CLU (Chartered Life Underwriter™) mean that your advisor has completed significant voluntary training beyond the basic licensing. They also mean that these professionals voluntarily adhere to the code of ethics and practice standards of the certifying organization. This by no means guarantees the person will be a competent and trustworthy advisor, but it does eliminate a lot of bad guys from your list. Remember, it's your life savings we're talking about. You can check out the designations of financial planners and insurance agents at designationcheck.com. For example, to find me, type in "North Carolina" and then my name, "Hans Scheil," and you'll find out what designations I hold, if I am in good standing, and when I earned them. To verify any CFP® go to LetsMakeAPlan.org and type in state and name and it comes right up.

In the first chapter of this book I laid out my personal values that guide my life and the retirement planning work we do at Cardinal: individual responsibility, the importance of personal growth, conscious decision making, open and honest communication, and the Golden Rule (treat others as you would be treated yourself).

Here I'll talk about how these values translate into the qualities and characteristics I think you should seek in a financial advisor and other professionals. For shorthand I refer to these features as: **Trust, Independence, Professional Designations, Verify, Fiduciary Standards, and Specialization.**

TRUST **in the advisor.** In any new relationship, I pay attention to my gut feelings and impressions. Do I like this person? Does he or she seem interested in serving me? Is this person talking down to me? Is he capable of listening and does he practice it? Do I get direct answers to my questions? Is she willing to provide references? How is he paid? Is the person a certified fiduciary (see below)?

You can talk with potential advisors over the phone as a way to do some initial screening. It may not be fair to make quick judgments, but remember, it is your life savings on the line; you are the customer. Tell the potential advisor you would like to spend fifteen to twenty minutes on the phone before deciding to meet with her. Ask your adult children, brother, or sister to help you with the calls if you are not comfortable making them by yourself.

INDEPENDENCE **from a big financial institution** is very important to me. If the name on the sign or website of the professional is a big insurance company, large bank, or national stock brokerage, be forewarned: Most of these institutions instruct their advisors to steer clients in a particular direction, toward their own products. But you can usually purchase the products of a large financial institution through an independent professional anyhow. I like to know that my advisors are recommending the best course of action for me vs. being sold the company sales pitch. Most attorneys and accountants in personal practice work independently and don't sell financial products.

VERIFY **the designations and the professional licenses.** You can type in "Hans Scheil" at the website of most state insurance departments, or at LetsMakeAPlan.org, FINRA's (Financial Industry Regulatory Authority) BrokerCheck, or OneFPA.org and check me out in about ten minutes. You (or your granddaughter or grandson) can do this on a cell phone or tablet.

A FIDUCIARY **standard of care** is much better than a simple suitability standard for you, the client. Investment advisors who charge fees for their services and Certified Financial Planners™ are bound to a fiduciary standard of care. We must be able to demonstrate that your needs are placed ahead of our own interests. The suitability standard is what most stockbrokers and insurance agents are held to. To prove suitability, the agent or broker must only show that what he sold you is appropriate for someone like you. The fiduciary oath—"I Am a Fiduciary and I Am Ready to Serve Retirement Investors"—contains the following pledges:

> I will put my client's best interest first.
> I will act with prudence; that is, with the skill, care, diligence and good
>   judgment of a professional.

I will not mislead clients and I will provide conspicuous, full, and fair disclosure of all important facts.

I will avoid conflicts of interest.

I will fully disclose and fairly manage, in my clients' favor, any unavoidable conflicts.

Look for **SPECIALIZATION of the practice in working with retired people**. Choose an insurance agent who writes a lot of Medicare Supplement policies, long-term care policies, life insurance policies, and annuities. Your financial advisor needs to know a lot about IRAs, Social Security, pension plans, annuities, estate planning, and taxes for people age 65 and older. Your CPA needs to work well with financial planners, insurance agents, and elder law attorneys. Similarly, your attorney should specialize in elder law and estate planning and work well with financial advisors, CPAs, and insurance agents.

———————•———————

Christina and Michael (see more of their story in chapter 4, page 32) were referred to me by an advisor assisting them with qualifying for veterans' benefits. Christina took in Michael (her father) after he had lived alone in Florida for ten years and slowly developed dementia. She found a nice assisted-living facility for him to live in. On the advice of the facility managers, Christina sought assistance in qualifying Michael for long-term care benefits through Veterans Aid and Attendance. The professional specializing in veterans she consulted charged her $1,000 up front with another $1,760 due when the VA benefit was awarded. He then referred Christina to an attorney to form a trust (suitable for the VA) to hold Michael's assets. The lawyer told Christina she could not form a trust until Michael filed his tax returns, which he had not done for the past ten years. The VA professional also referred Christina to his accountant, who works out of her house. The accountant became sick soon after, and before Christina knew it, a year had passed. There is a similar story too long to tell involving the insurance advisor he referred Christina to.

Cardinal was brought in by the VA professional to help clean up the financial mess. We had the tax returns on the mend only to learn that Christina could have applied for Veterans Aid and Attendance without filing them. And we hired a new attorney who completed the trust. Michael's financial institutions would not accept Christina's power of attorney because it was not registered properly.

The cautionary tale here is about the malpractice of this VA-accredited agent. He referred Christina to a lawyer, a CPA, and a financial advisor/insurance agent who did nothing to help her. He did not follow up with the other professionals or with Christina and left the financial planning, tax returns, and legal documents in limbo for over a year. This lack of professionalism really angers me, especially when perpetrated against vulnerable older people. I recommend finding a CFP® professional who specializes in eldercare planning and estate planning and putting her or him in charge of coordinating and even finding the other professionals. If you give me a call, write me a letter, or send me an email, I will serve you myself or help you locate competent professionals in your area.

Choose an insurance agent and/or financial planner who proudly displays CFP®, CLU®, CASL®, CPA, JD, or ChFC® after his or her name. It means that person has completed an extensive course of study, kept current with emerging rules and trends, and most importantly, adheres to a strict code of ethics. The CFP® code of ethics requires a CFP® to practice with integrity, objectivity, competence, fairness, confidentiality, professionalism, and diligence. The other professional designations in the list hold their members to a similar code of ethics. However, you also need to be on the lookout for designations that sound similar but are not the same. Many lookalikes are out there but they are not the same. In fact, some states have outlawed the use of lookalike designations for professionals who consult with seniors.

———◆———

I hope you have found the information presented in this book to be helpful and enlightening. I hope I've persuaded you of the serious importance of financial planning for retirement, and that there's a right way to do it, with the guidance of experienced and competent professionals. And I hope I've opened your eyes to potential complications and problems to be aware of as you go through the retirement planning process. Cardinal stands ready to offer you our services, and I look forward to hearing from you.

SUMMARY: CHOOSING THE RIGHT ADVISOR

- Find a CFP (Certified Financial Planner™) who specializes in eldercare planning and estate planning. You can start at LetsMakeAPlan.org.

- A CFP® can help you locate an elder law attorney, an estate planning attorney, and/or a CPA if needed.

- Buy your insurance from an independent agent who represents several insurance companies and specializes in insurance products appropriate for seniors.

- Our Cardinal principles are: Trust, Independence, Professional Designations, Verify, Fiduciary Standards, and Specialization.

APPENDIX A | SOCIAL SECURITY EARNINGS REPORT

This is my (author Hans Scheil's) personal Social Security earnings statement. You can get your own at http://socialsecurity.gov. On page 4, the Social Security Administration recommends looking into long-term care insurance because Medicare pays little for long-term care.

Prevent identity theft—protect your Social Security number

Your Social Security Statement

www.socialsecurity.gov

February 13, 2015

See inside for your personal information ➡

What's inside...

What Social Security Means To You

This *Social Security Statement* can help you plan for your financial future. It provides estimates of your Social Security benefits under current law and updates your latest reported earnings.

Please read this *Statement* carefully. If you see a mistake, please let us know. That's important because your benefits will be based on our record of your lifetime earnings. We recommend you keep a copy of your *Statement* with your financial records.

Social Security is for people of all ages...
We're more than a retirement program. Social Security also can provide benefits if you become disabled and help support your family after you die.

Work to build a secure future...
Social Security is the largest source of income for most elderly Americans today, but Social Security was never intended to be your only source of income when you retire. You also will need other savings, investments, pensions or retirement accounts to make sure you have enough money to live comfortably when you retire.

Saving and investing wisely are important not only for you and your family, but for the entire country. If you want to learn more about how and why to save, you should visit *www.mymoney.gov*, a federal government website dedicated to teaching all Americans the basics of financial management.

About Social Security's future...
Social Security is a compact between generations. Since 1935, America has kept the promise of security for its workers and their families. Now, however, the Social Security system is facing serious financial problems, and action is needed soon to make sure the system will be sound when today's younger workers are ready for retirement.

Without changes, in 2033 the Social Security Trust Fund will be able to pay only about 77 cents for each dollar of scheduled benefits.* We need to resolve these issues soon to make sure Social Security continues to provide a foundation of protection for future generations.

Social Security on the Net...
You can read publications, including *When To Start Receiving Retirement Benefits*; use our Retirement Estimator to obtain immediate and personalized estimates of future benefits; and when you're ready to apply for benefits, use our improved online application—It's so easy!

Carolyn W. Colvin
Carolyn W. Colvin
Acting Commissioner

* These estimates are based on the intermediate assumptions from the Social Security Trustees' Annual Report to the Congress.

Your Estimated Benefits

*Retirement	You have earned enough credits to qualify for benefits. At your current earnings rate, if you continue working until...	
	your full retirement age (66 and 8 months), your payment would be about	$ 2,570 a month
	age 70, your payment would be about	$ 3,255 a month
	age 62, your payment would be about	$ 1,842 a month
*Disability	You have earned enough credits to qualify for benefits. If you became disabled right now your payment would be about	$ 2,657 a month
*Family	If you get retirement or disability benefits, your spouse and children also may qualify for benefits.	
*Survivors	You have earned enough credits for your family to receive survivors benefits. If you die this year, certain members of your family may qualify for the following benefits:	
	Your child	$ 1,992 a month
	Your spouse who is caring for your child	$ 1,992 a month
	Your spouse, if benefits start at full retirement age	$ 2,657 a month
	Total family benefits cannot be more than	$ 4,649 a month
	Your spouse or minor child may be eligible for a special one-time death benefit of $255.	
Medicare	You have enough credits to qualify for Medicare at age 65. Even if you do not retire at age 65, be sure to contact Social Security three months before your 65th birthday to enroll in Medicare.	

* **Your estimated benefits are based on current law. Congress has made changes to the law in the past and can do so at any time. The law governing benefit amounts may change because, by 2033, the payroll taxes collected will be enough to pay only about 77 percent of scheduled benefits.**

We based your benefit estimates on these facts:
Your date of birth (please verify your name on page 1 and this date of birth) ....
Your estimated taxable earnings per year after 2015 ....
Your Social Security number (only the last four digits are shown to help prevent identity theft) ....

How Your Benefits Are Estimated

To qualify for benefits, you earn "credits" through your work — up to four each year. This year, for example, you earn one credit for each $1,220 of wages or self-employment income. When you've earned $4,880, you've earned your four credits for the year. Most people need 40 credits, earned over their working lifetime, to receive retirement benefits. For disability and survivors benefits, young people need fewer credits to be eligible.

We checked your records to see whether you have earned enough credits to qualify for benefits. If you haven't earned enough yet to qualify for any type of benefit, we can't give you a benefit estimate now. If you continue to work, we'll give you an estimate when you do qualify.

What we assumed — If you have enough work credits, we estimated your benefit amounts using your average earnings over your working lifetime. For 2015 and later (up to retirement age), we assumed you'll continue to work and make about the same as you did in 2013 or 2014. We also included credits we assumed you earned last year and this year.

Generally, the older you are and the closer you are to retirement, the more accurate the retirement estimates will be because they are based on a longer work history with fewer uncertainties such as earnings fluctuations and future law changes. We encourage you to use our online Retirement Estimator to obtain immediate and personalized benefit estimates.

We can't provide your actual benefit amount until you apply for benefits. **And that amount may differ from the estimates above because:**

(1) Your earnings may increase or decrease in the future.
(2) After you start receiving benefits, they will be adjusted for cost-of-living increases.

(3) Your estimated benefits are based on current law. **The law governing benefit amounts may change.**
(4) Your benefit amount may be affected by **military service, railroad employment or pensions earned through work on which you did not pay Social Security tax.** Visit *www.socialsecurity.gov* to learn more.

Windfall Elimination Provision (WEP) — If you receive a pension from employment in which you did not pay Social Security taxes and you also qualify for your own Social Security retirement or disability benefit, your Social Security benefit may be reduced, but not eliminated, by WEP. The amount of the reduction, if any, depends on your earnings and number of years in jobs in which you paid Social Security taxes, and the year you are age 62 or become disabled. To estimate WEP's effect on your Social Security benefit, visit *www.socialsecurity.gov/WEP-CHART*. In 2015, the maximum monthly reduction is $413. For more information, please see *Windfall Elimination Provision* (Publication No. 05-10045) at *www.socialsecurity.gov/WEP*.

Government Pension Offset (GPO) — If you receive a pension based on federal, state or local government work in which you did not pay Social Security taxes and you qualify, now or in the future, for Social Security benefits as a current or former spouse, widow or widower, you are likely to be affected by GPO. If GPO applies, your Social Security benefit will be reduced by an amount equal to two-thirds of your government pension, and could be reduced to zero. Even if your benefit is reduced to zero, you will be eligible for Medicare at age 65 on your spouse's record. To learn more, please see *Government Pension Offset* (Publication No. 05-10007) at *www.socialsecurity.gov/GPO*.

Your Earnings Record

Years You Worked	Your Taxed Social Security Earnings	Your Taxed Medicare Earnings		Years You Worked	Your Taxed Social Security Earnings	Your Taxed Medicare Earnings
1977	1,669	1,669		2008	102,000	961,766
1978	3,071	3,071		2009	106,800	686,369
1979	3,620	3,620				
				2010	106,800	290,089
1980	3,844	3,844				
1981	18,462	18,462				
1982	20,902	20,902				
1983	26,864	26,864				
1984	37,800	37,800				
1985	39,600	39,600				
1986	42,000	42,000				
1987	43,800	43,800				
1988	45,000	45,000				
1989	48,000	48,000				
1990	51,300	51,300				
1991	53,400	89,821				
1992	45,968	45,968				
1993	57,600	111,345				
1994	60,600	91,266				
1995	61,200	128,285				
1996	62,700	149,537				
1997	65,400	171,501				
1998	68,400	307,914				
1999	72,600	404,038				
2000	76,200	618,632				
2001	80,400	867,428				
2002	84,900	803,068				
2003	87,000	740,885				
2004	87,900	702,210				
2005	90,000	843,896				
2006	94,200	950,398				
2007	97,500	832,832				

Total Social Security and Medicare taxes paid over your working career through the last year reported on the chart above:

Estimated taxes paid for Social Security:		Estimated taxes paid for Medicare:	
You paid:	$127,177	You paid:	$149,951
Your employers paid:	$134,375	Your employers paid:	$149,883

Note: Currently, you and your employer each pay a 6.2 percent Social Security tax on up to $118,500 of your earnings and a 1.45 percent Medicare tax on all your earnings. If you are self-employed, you pay the combined employee and employer amount, which is a 12.4 percent Social Security tax on up to $118,500 of your net earnings and a 2.9 percent Medicare tax on your entire net earnings. If you have earned income of more than $200,000 ($250,000 for married couples filing jointly), you must pay 0.9 percent more in Medicare taxes.

Help Us Keep Your Earnings Record Accurate

You, your employer and Social Security share responsibility for the accuracy of your earnings record. Since you began working, we recorded your reported earnings under your name and Social Security number. We have updated your record each time your employer (or you, if you're self-employed) reported your earnings.

Remember, it's your earnings, not the amount of taxes you paid or the number of credits you've earned, that determine your benefit amount. When we figure that amount, we base it on your average earnings over your lifetime. If our records are wrong, you may not receive all the benefits to which you're entitled.

Review this chart carefully using your own records to make sure our information is correct and that we've recorded each year you worked. You're the only person who can look at the earnings chart and know whether it is complete and correct.

Some or all of your earnings from **last year** may not be shown on your *Statement*. It could be that we still were processing last year's earnings reports when your *Statement* was prepared. **Note:** If you worked for more than one employer during any year, or if you had both earnings and self-employment income, we combined your earnings for the year.

There's a limit on the amount of earnings on which you pay Social Security taxes each year. The limit increases yearly. Earnings above the limit will not appear on your earnings chart as Social Security earnings. (For Medicare taxes, the maximum earnings amount began rising in 1991. Since 1994, **all** of your earnings are taxed for Medicare.)

Call us right away at **1-800-772-1213** (7 a.m.-7 p.m. your local time) if any earnings for years **before last year** are shown incorrectly. Please have your W-2 or tax return for those years available. (If you live outside the U.S., follow the directions at the bottom of page 4.)

Some Facts About Social Security

About Social Security and Medicare...

Social Security pays retirement, disability, family and survivors benefits. Medicare, a separate program run by the Centers for Medicare & Medicaid Services, helps pay for inpatient hospital care, nursing care, doctors' fees, drugs, and other medical services and supplies to people age 65 and older, as well as to people who have been receiving Social Security disability benefits for two years or more. Medicare does not pay for long-term care, so you may want to consider options for private insurance. Your Social Security covered earnings qualify you for both programs. For more information about Medicare, visit *www.medicare.gov* or call **1-800-633-4227** (TTY **1-877-486-2048** if you are deaf or hard of hearing).

Retirement — If you were born before 1938, your full retirement age is 65. Because of a 1983 change in the law, the full retirement age will increase gradually to 67 for people born in 1960 and later.

Some people retire before their full retirement age. You can retire as early as 62 and take benefits at a reduced rate. If you work after your full retirement age, you can receive higher benefits because of additional earnings and credits for delayed retirement.

Disability — If you become disabled before full retirement age, you can receive disability benefits after six months if you have:
— enough credits from earnings (depending on your age, you must have earned six to 20 of your credits in the three to 10 years before you became disabled); and
— a physical or mental impairment that's expected to prevent you from doing "substantial" work for a year or more *or* result in death.

If you are filing for disability benefits, please let us know if you are on active military duty or are a recently discharged veteran, so that we can handle your claim more quickly.

Family — If you're eligible for disability or retirement benefits, your current or divorced spouse, minor children or adult children disabled before age 22 also may receive benefits. Each may qualify for up to about 50 percent of your benefit amount.

Survivors — When you die, certain members of your family may be eligible for benefits:
—your spouse age 60 or older (50 or older if disabled, or any age if caring for your children younger than age 16); and
—your children if unmarried and younger than age 18, still in school and younger than 19 years old, or adult children disabled before age 22.

If you are divorced, your ex-spouse could be eligible for a widow's or widower's benefit on your record when you die.

Extra Help with Medicare — If you know someone who is on Medicare and has limited income and resources, extra help is available for prescription drug costs. The extra help can help pay the monthly premiums, annual deductibles and prescription co-payments. To learn more or to apply, visit *www.socialsecurity.gov* or call **1-800-772-1213** (TTY **1-800-325-0778**).

Receive benefits and still work...

You can work and still get retirement or survivors benefits. If you're younger than your full retirement age, there are limits on how much you can earn without affecting your benefit amount. When you apply for benefits, we'll tell you what the limits are and whether work would affect your monthly benefits. When you reach full retirement age, the earnings limits no longer apply.

Before you decide to retire...

Carefully consider the advantages and disadvantages of early retirement. If you choose to receive benefits before you reach full retirement age, your monthly benefits will be reduced.

To help you decide the best time to retire, we offer a free publication, *When To Start Receiving Retirement Benefits* (Publication No. 05-10147), that identifies the many factors you should consider before applying. Most people can receive an estimate of their benefit based on their actual Social Security earnings record by using our online Retirement Estimator. You also can calculate future retirement benefits by using the Social Security Benefit Calculators at *www.socialsecurity.gov*.

Other helpful free publications include:
— *Retirement Benefits* (No. 05-10035)
— *Understanding The Benefits* (No. 05-10024)
— *Your Retirement Benefit: How It Is Figured* (No. 05-10070)
— *Windfall Elimination Provision* (No. 05-10045)
— *Government Pension Offset* (No. 05-10007)
— *Identity Theft And Your Social Security Number* (No. 05-10064)

We also have other leaflets and fact sheets with information about specific topics such as military service, self-employment or foreign employment. You can request Social Security publications at our website, *www.socialsecurity.gov*, or by calling us at **1-800-772-1213**. Our website has a list of frequently asked questions that may answer questions you have. We have easy-to-use online applications for benefits that can save you a telephone call or a trip to a field office.

You may also qualify for government benefits outside of Social Security. For more information on these benefits, visit *www.govbenefits.gov*.

If you need more information — Contact any Social Security office, or call us toll-free at **1-800-772-1213**. (If you are deaf or hard of hearing, you may call our TTY number, **1-800-325-0778**.) If you have questions about your personal information, you must provide your complete Social Security Number. If you are in the United States, you also may write to the Social Security Administration, Office of Earnings Operations, P.O. Box 33026, Baltimore, MD 21290-3026. If you are outside the United States, please write to the Office of International Operations, P.O. Box 17769, Baltimore, MD 21235-7769, USA.

APPENDIX B | VARIATION IN MEDICARE SUPPLEMENT PLAN PREMIUMS

These two reports show the price for Medicare Supplement Plans F and G charged by several insurance companies for THE EXACT SAME POLICY. In both cases, the highest premium is more than twice as expensive as the lowest one.

Female - Age 70 - Non-Tobacco - North Carolina - 27511 - Plan F: 07/01/2015			
CSI Life	$119.42	Thrivent Financial	$173.25
Old Surety	$119.79	Columbian Mutual	$177.80
Aetna Health and Life	$130.45	Equitable Life	$187.25
Medico Corp	$131.37	Globe Life	$189.00
GPM Life	$135.05	State Mutual	$189.42
Central States Indemnity	$135.17	Bankers Fidelity	$196.00
New Era Life	$135.21	American Republic Corp	$197.60
HumanaDental	$135.36	Gerber Life	$197.95
IAC	$135.53	BCBS of North Carolina	$200.50
Manhattan Life	$137.17	Reserve National	$206.25
American Republic	$139.14	Humana	$208.60
Combined	$139.40	Humana	$213.96
Equitable Life	$140.58	Sterling Life	$219.77
American Retirement Life Ins	$141.74	Colonial Penn	$220.68
Oxford Life	$144.65	Sterling Life	$224.63
Mutual of Omaha	$148.14	United American	$235.00
USAA Life	$148.41	Reserve National	$237.20
Sentinel Security	$161.09	Standard Life and Acc	$238.28
American Republic	$163.69	Colonial Penn	$245.09
American Republic Corp	$167.96	Physicians Mutual	$245.66
State Farm	$170.93	United Commercial Travelers	$246.28
UnitedHealthcare	$173.10	UnitedHealthcare	$260.65
Aetna Life	$173.16	Colonial Penn	$272.21

Disclaimer: CSG Actuarial, LLC does not guarantee or warrant the accuracy of the above premium rates or underwriting information. Carriers may have made rate or underwriting adjustments that have not yet been reflected in our database. All data obtained from public sources.

A few companies in the database offer premium rates based upon special underwriting or administrative rules. In those cases multiple rates are shown for the same company.

2013 Market Data Source: 2013 NAIC Medicare Supplement Experience Exhibits and data filed with the National Association of Insurance Commissioners in annual financial statements. CSG Actuarial, LLC does not guarantee or warrant the accuracy of the above market data.

Female - Age 70 - Non-Tobacco - North Carolina - 27511 -Plan G: 07/01/2015

CSI Life	$94.17	Bankers Fidelity	$145.00
Mutual of Omaha	$104.36	Thrivent Financial	$152.46
Equitable Life	$108.35	Aetna Life	$161.16
GPM Life	$108.66	State Mutual	$162.25
Central States Indemnity	$110.25	Gerber Life	$166.90
New Era Life	$110.38	Colonial Penn	$171.26
IAC	$112.08	Standard Life and Acc	$175.93
HumanaDental	$114.96	United Commercial Travelers	$184.86
Manhattan Life	$116.25	Sterling Life	$189.23
Aetna Health and Life	$121.37	Colonial Penn	$190.18
Medico Corp	$121.88	BCBS of North Carolina	$191.50
American Retirement Life Ins	$124.01	Physicians Mutual	$192.94
Columbian Mutual	$141.96	Colonial Penn	$211.20
Equitable Life	$144.43	United American	$222.00
		Physicians Mutual	$223.40

Disclaimer: CSG Actuarial, LLC does not guarantee or warrant the accuracy of the above premium rates or under-writing information. Carriers may have made rate or underwriting adjustments that have not yet been reflected in our database. All data obtained from public sources.

A few companies in the database offer premium rates based upon special underwriting or administrative rules. In those cases multiple rates are shown for the same company.

2013 Market Data Source: 2013 NAIC Medicare Supplement Experience Exhibits and data filed with the National Association of Insurance Commissioners in annual financial statements. CSG Actuarial, LLC does not guarantee or warrant the accuracy of the above market data.

APPENDIX C | # VETERANS ADMINISTRATION FOR VETERANS AID AND ATTENDANCE

This is a copy of the approval letter from the Veterans Administration for Veterans Aid and Attendance for one of our Cardinal clients.

DEPARTMENT OF VETERANS AFFAIRS
VARO Philadelphia
5000 WISSAHICKON AVENUE
PO Box 8709
PHILADELPHIA PA 19101

MAY 29 2015

Dear Mr.

We made a decision on your claim received April 16, 2015. Your claim was processed under the Fully Developed Claim Program.

This letter tells you about your entitlement amount, payment start date, what we decided, and how we calculated your benefits. It also tells you of your responsibilities as a veteran in receipt of disability pension, what to do if you disagree with our decision, and who to contact if you have questions or need assistance.

Your Award Amount and Payment Start Date

Your monthly entitlement amount is shown below:

Total VA Benefit	Amount Withheld	Amount Paid	Effective Date	Reason For Change
$1,788.00	$1,788.00	$0.00	May 1, 2015	Pension Grant With Aid and Attendance - Withholding Pending Appointment of Fiduciary
1,788.00	0.00	1,788.00	Jun 1, 2015	Funds Released, Pending Appointment of Fiduciary

We are paying you as a single veteran with no dependents.

We Have Withheld Benefits

We are withholding your benefits pending an appointment of a custodian because of your diagnosis of mental incompetence. You will receive a letter regarding this.

What We Decided

We granted disability pension benefits with aid and attendance effective April 16, 2015.

2

We have enclosed a copy of your Rating Decision for your review. It provides a detailed explanation of our decision, the evidence considered, and the reasons for our decision. Your Rating Decision and this letter constitute our decision based on your claim received on April 16, 2015. It represents all claims we understood to be specifically made, implied, or inferred in that claim.

We enclosed a VA Form 21-8768, "Disability Pension Award Attachment" which explains important factors concerning your benefits.

What Income And Expenses Did We Use?

We used your total family income as shown below to award your pension benefit from May 1, 2015.

Income We Counted

	Annual Long Term Care Ins.	Annual Social Security	Annual Retirement	Annual Interest
Yourself	$36,951.00	$19,894.00	$8,373.00	$12.00

We used your medical expenses of $66,106.00 which represents the amount you pay for assisted living fees and Medicare (part B) as a continuing deduction from May 1, 2015. This reduces your countable income to $0.00. If the amount you pay for medical expenses changes or you are no longer paying medical expenses, tell us immediately. If you don't tell us about changes in your medical expenses, we may pay you too much money. You would have to pay back this money.

What Are Your Responsibilities?

You are responsible to tell us right away if:

- your income or the income of your dependents changes (e.g., earnings, Social Security benefits, lottery and gambling winnings)
- your net worth increases (e.g., bank accounts, investments, real estate)
- your continuing medical expenses are reduced
- you gain or lose a dependent
- your address or phone number changes

APPENDIX D | **MEDICARE SURCHARGES**

This letter from Medicare explains the imposition of surcharges on one of our clients for Medicare Part B and Part D.

Social Security Administration

Date: November 26, 2014
Claim Number:

Your Social Security benefits will increase by 1.7 percent in 2015 because of a rise in the cost of living. The Social Security Act requires some people to pay higher premiums for their Medicare Part B (Medical Insurance) and their prescription drug coverage based on their income. Because of your income, your premiums will be increased. The information in this notice about your premium is for 2015 only.

If you currently do not have Medicare Part B or prescription drug coverage and enroll in 2015, those premiums will also be increased based on your income.

How Much Social Security Will I Get?

- Your new 2015 monthly benefit
  amount before deductions is: $1,558.70

- Your 2015 monthly deduction for the
  Medicare Part B Premium is: - $272.70

  - $104.90 for the standard Medicare premium, plus

  - $167.80 for the income-related monthly adjustment amount based on
    your 2012 income tax return

- Your 2015 deduction for prescription drug coverage is: - $38.30

Your 2015 deduction for
Medicare Advantage is: - $26.10

- Your 2015 deduction for prescription drug coverage income-related
  monthly adjustment amount based on your 2012 income tax return is:
     - $51.30

- Your benefit amount after deductions
  that will be deposited into your bank account
  or sent in your check on January 21, 2015 is: $1,170.30

APPENDIX E | MORNINGSTAR REPORT

The Morningstar report provides an independent analysis of your investments. We include a personalized Morningstar report in our financial plans.

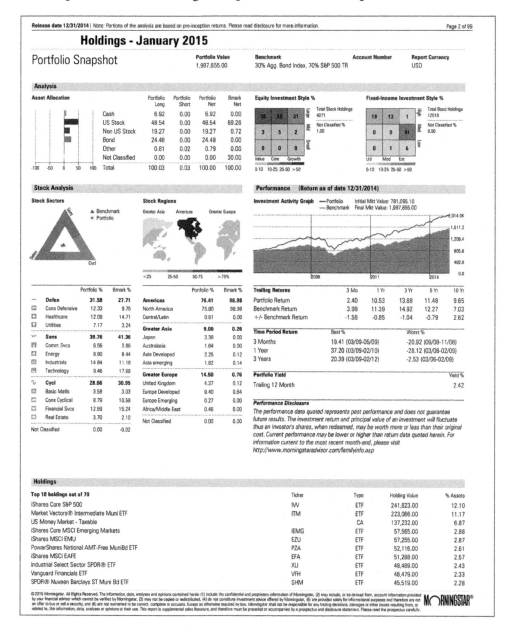

Release date 12/31/2014 | Note: Portions of the analysis are based on pre-inception returns. Please read disclosure for more information.

Holdings - January 2015

Portfolio Snapshot

Portfolio Value	Benchmark	Account Number	Report Currency
1,997,655.00	30% Agg. Bond Index, 70% S&P 500 TR		USD

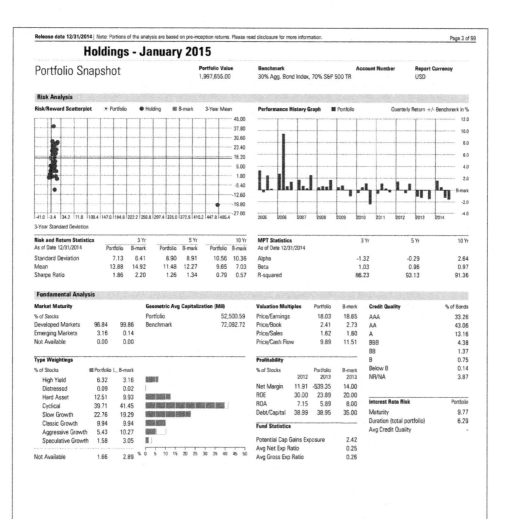

Risk Analysis

Risk/Reward Scatterplot ● Portfolio ● Holding ■ B-mark   3-Year Mean

3-Year Standard Deviation

Performance History Graph ■ Portfolio   Quarterly Return +/- Benchmark in %

Risk and Return Statistics		3 Yr		5 Yr		10 Yr	
As of Date 12/31/2014	Portfolio	B-mark	Portfolio	B-mark	Portfolio	B-mark
Standard Deviation	7.13	6.41	8.90	8.91	10.56	10.36
Mean	13.88	14.92	11.48	12.27	9.65	7.03
Sharpe Ratio	1.86	2.20	1.26	1.34	0.79	0.57

MPT Statistics	3 Yr	5 Yr	10 Yr
As of Date 12/31/2014			
Alpha	-1.32	-0.29	2.64
Beta	1.03	0.95	0.97
R-squared	86.23	93.13	91.36

Fundamental Analysis

Market Maturity

% of Stocks		
Developed Markets	96.84	99.86
Emerging Markets	3.16	0.14
Not Available	0.00	0.00

Geometric Avg Capitalization (Mil)

Portfolio	52,500.59
Benchmark	72,092.72

Valuation Multiples	Portfolio	B-mark
Price/Earnings	18.03	18.65
Price/Book	2.41	2.73
Price/Sales	1.62	1.80
Price/Cash Flow	9.89	11.51

Credit Quality	% of Bonds
AAA	33.26
AA	43.06
A	13.16
BBB	4.38
BB	1.37
B	0.75
Below B	0.14
NR/NA	3.87

Type Weightings

% of Stocks	■ Portfolio	L_ B-mark	
High Yield	6.32	3.16	
Distressed	0.09	0.02	
Hard Asset	12.51	9.93	
Cyclical	39.71	41.45	
Slow Growth	22.76	19.29	
Classic Growth	9.94	9.94	
Aggressive Growth	5.43	10.27	
Speculative Growth	1.58	3.05	
Not Available	1.66	2.89	

% 0 5 10 15 20 25 30 35 40 45 50

Profitability

% of Stocks	2012	Portfolio 2013	B-mark 2013
Net Margin	11.91	-539.35	14.00
ROE	30.00	23.89	20.00
ROA	7.15	5.89	8.00
Debt/Capital	38.99	38.95	35.00

Fund Statistics

Potential Cap Gains Exposure	2.42
Avg Net Exp Ratio	0.25
Avg Gross Exp Ratio	0.26

Interest Rate Risk	Portfolio
Maturity	9.77
Duration (total portfolio)	6.29
Avg Credit Quality	-

 MORNINGSTAR®

APPENDIX F | SAMPLE POWER OF ATTORNEY

An example of a power of attorney document in North Carolina.

Chapter 32A.

Powers of Attorney.

Article 1.

Statutory Short Form Power of Attorney.

§ 32A-1. Statutory Short Form of General Power of Attorney.

The use of the following form in the creation of a power of attorney is lawful, and, when used, it shall be construed in accordance with the provisions of this Chapter.

"NOTICE: THE POWERS GRANTED BY THIS DOCUMENT ARE BROAD AND SWEEPING. THEY ARE DEFINED IN CHAPTER 32A OF THE NORTH CAROLINA GENERAL STATUTES WHICH EXPRESSLY PERMITS THE USE OF ANY OTHER OR DIFFERENT FORM OF POWER OF ATTORNEY DESIRED BY THE PARTIES CONCERNED.

State of _____.

County of _____.

I _____, appoint _____ to be my attorney-in-fact, to act in my name in any way which I could act for myself, with respect to the following matters as each of them is defined in Chapter 32A of the North Carolina General Statutes. (DIRECTIONS: Initial the line opposite any one or more of the subdivisions as to which the principal desires to give the attorney-in-fact authority.)

(1)	Real property transactions	_____
(2)	Personal property transactions	_____
(3)	Bond, share, stock, securities and commodity transactions	_____
(4)	Banking transactions	_____
(5)	Safe deposits	_____
(6)	Business operating transactions	_____
(7)	Insurance transactions	_____
(8)	Estate transactions	_____
(9)	Personal relationships and affairs	_____
(10)	Social security and unemployment	_____
(11)	Benefits from military service	_____
(12)	Tax matters	_____
(13)	Employment of agents	_____
(14)	Gifts to charities, and to individuals other than the attorney-in-fact	_____
(15)	Gifts to the named attorney-in-fact	_____
(16)	Renunciation of an interest in or power over property to benefit persons other than the attorney-in-fact	_____
(17)	Renunciation of an interest in or power over property to benefit persons including the attorney-in-fact	_____

(If power of substitution and revocation is to be given, add: 'I also give to such person full power to appoint another to act as my attorney-in-fact and full power to revoke such appointment.')

(If period of power of attorney is to be limited, add: "This power terminates ____, ___')

(If power of attorney is to be a durable power of attorney under the provision of Article 2 of Chapter 32A and is to continue in effect after the incapacity or mental incompetence of the principal, add: 'This power of attorney shall not be affected by my subsequent incapacity or mental incompetence.')

G.S. 32A-1   Page 1

(If power of attorney is to take effect only after the incapacity or mental incompetence of the principal, add: 'This power of attorney shall become effective after I become incapacitated or mentally incompetent.')

(If power of attorney is to be effective to terminate or direct the administration of a custodial trust created under the Uniform Custodial Trust Act, add: 'In the event of my subsequent incapacity or mental incompetence, the attorney-in-fact of this power of attorney shall have the power to terminate or to direct the administration of any custodial trust of which I am the beneficiary.')

(If power of attorney is to be effective to determine whether a beneficiary under the Uniform Custodial Trust Act is incapacitated or ceases to be incapacitated, add: 'The attorney-in-fact of this power of attorney shall have the power to determine whether I am incapacitated or whether my incapacity has ceased for the purposes of any custodial trust of which I am the beneficiary.')

Dated_____, _____ .

_____ (Seal)
Signature

STATE OF _____ COUNTY OF _____

On this _____ day of_____, _____, personally appeared before me, the said named _____ to me known and known to me to be the person described in and who executed the foregoing instrument and he (or she) acknowledged that he (or she) executed the same and being duly sworn by me, made oath that the statements in the foregoing instrument are true.

My Commission Expires _____.

_____
(Signature of Notary Public)
Notary Public (Official Seal)"

(1983, c. 626, s. 1; 1985, c. 162, s. 1; c. 618, s. 1; 1995, c. 331, s. 1; c. 486, s. 2; 2009-48, s. 11.)

APPENDIX G | **SAMPLE HIPAA RELEASE**

An example of a HIPAA release form.

Medical Information Release Form

(HIPAA Release Form)

Name: _____ Date of Birth: _____/____/_____

Release of Information

[ ]   I authorize the release of information including the diagnosis, records; examination rendered to me and claims information. This information may be released to:

     [ ] Spouse_____

     [ ] Child(ren)_____

     [ ] Other_____

[ ]   Information is not to be released to anyone.

This **Release of Information** will remain in effect until terminated by me in writing.

Messages

Please call   [ ] my home   [ ] my work   [ ] my cell Number:_____

If unable to reach me:

     [ ] you may leave a detailed message

     [ ] please leave a message asking me to return your call

     [ ] _____

The best time to reach me is (*day*)_____ between (*time*)_____

Signed: _____ Date: ____/____/_____

Witness:_____ Date: ___/____/_____

APPENDIX H | **1926 TAX RETURN**

Notice the exemptions on this 1926 tax return. Death proceeds from life insurance policies have been income tax free for beneficiaries for a long time. This exemption remains in effect today.

STATEMENT OF CONTRIBUTIONS

NAME OF ORGANIZATION	AMOUNT PAID	NAME OF ORGANIZATION	AMOUNT PAID
Pres. Church	$ 53 00	*Pres. Church Sunday School*	$ 30 00
Y M C A	18 00		$

NONTAXABLE OBLIGATIONS AND SECURITIES

OBLIGATIONS AND SECURITIES	AMOUNT OWNED	INTEREST RECEIVED
(a) Obligations of a State, Territory, or political subdivision thereof, or the District of Columbia.	$	$
(b) Securities issued under the Federal Farm Loan Act, or under such Act as amended.		
(c) Obligations of the United States or its possessions.		

AFFIDAVIT

I swear (or affirm) that this return has been examined by me, and, to the best of my knowledge and belief, is a true and complete return for the taxable year as stated, pursuant to the Revenue Act of 1926 and Regulations issued under authority thereof.

(If return is made by agent, the reason therefor must be stated on this line)

Sworn to and subscribed before me this

_____
(Signature of taxpayer or agent)

_____ day of _____, 1927

_____
(Address of agent)

_____
(Signature of officer administering oath)   (Title)

INSTRUCTIONS

Liability for Filing Return

An income tax return must be filed by every citizen of the United States whether residing at home or abroad, and every person residing in the United States, though not a citizen thereof, having a gross income for the calendar year 1926 of $5,000 or over, or a net income for the same period of (a) $1,500 or over, if single, or if married and not living with husband or wife, or (b) $3,500 or over, if married and living with husband or wife, or (c) regardless of amount if the net income exceeds the personal exemption.

Items Exempt from Tax

(a) Amounts received under a life insurance contract paid by reason of the death of the insured.
(b) Amounts received (other than by reason of the death of the insured) under a life insurance, endowment, or annuity contract, not to exceed the premiums or consideration paid for such contract.
(c) Gifts (not made as a consideration for services), and property acquired by bequest, devise, or inheritance (but the income from such property is taxable and must be reported).
(d) Interest upon (a) obligations of a State, Territory, or a political subdivision thereof, or the District of Columbia; (b) Federal Farm Loan bonds; and (c) all obligations of the United States and its possessions as to normal tax. Interest on Liberty Bonds owned in excess of $5,000 is subject to surtax if the net income is over $10,000.
(e) Amounts received as accident or health insurance for personal injuries or sickness, plus damages received on account of such injuries or sickness.
(f) Amounts received under the War Risk Insurance and Vocational Rehabilitation Acts, or the World War Veterans' Act, 1924, or as pensions from the United States for services in the military or naval forces in time of war, or as a State pension for services rendered for which the State is paying a pension.
(g) Dividends or interest, not exceeding $300, received from domestic building and loan associations, substantially all the business of which is confined to making loans to members.
(h) Rental value of a dwelling house and appurtenances thereof furnished a minister of the gospel as part of his compensation.
(i) Compensation paid by a State or political subdivision thereof to its officers or employees.
(j) Compensation received from sources without the United States by a citizen who is a nonresident for more than six months of the taxable year.

Personal Exemption and Credits

A single person, or a married person not living with husband or wife, may claim a personal exemption of $1,500. A person who, during the entire taxable year, was the head of a family or was married and living with husband or wife, may claim an exemption of $3,500.
A "head of a family" is an individual who actually supports and maintains in one household one or more individuals who are closely connected with him by blood relationship, relationship by marriage, or by adoption, and whose right to exercise family control and provide for these dependent individuals is based upon some moral or legal obligation.
If husband and wife file separate returns, the personal exemption may be taken by either or divided between them. In addition to the personal exemption, a credit of $400 may be claimed for each person (other than husband or wife) under eighteen years of age, or incapable of self-support because mentally or physically defective, who was receiving his or her chief support from the taxpayer on the last day of the taxable year. This credit can be claimed only by the person who furnishes the chief support, and can not be divided between two individuals.
In case the status of a taxpayer changes during the taxable year, the personal exemption shall be an amount which bears the same ratio to $1,500 as the number of months during which the taxpayer was single bears to twelve months, plus an amount which bears the same ratio to $3,500 as the number of months during which the taxpayer was married and living with husband or wife, or was the head of a family, bears to twelve months. For this purpose a fractional part of a month shall be disregarded unless it amounts to more than half a month, in which case it shall be considered as a full month. The amount of personal exemption shall not exceed $3,500 where the head of a family is married during the taxable year.
In the case of an individual who dies during the taxable year, the credits for personal exemption and dependents shall be determined by his or her status at the time of death. Full credits shall also be allowed to the surviving spouse according to his or her status at the close of the taxable year.

General Information

Affidavit.—The oath will be administered without charge by any collector, deputy collector, or internal revenue agent.
Returns.—File the return with the Collector of Internal Revenue for the district in which you reside on or before March 15, 1927.
Tax.—The tax may be paid at time of filing the return, or in four equal installments payable quarterly.
Penalties.—The following penalties are imposed by the statute:
For wilful failure to make and file a return on time, not more than $10,000 or imprisonment for not more than one year, or both, and, in addition, 25 per cent of the amount of the tax;
For wilfully making a false or fraudulent return, not more than $10,000 or imprisonment for not more than five years, or both, and, in addition, 50 per cent of the amount of the tax; and
For deficiency in tax, interest on deficiency at 6 per cent per annum to the date the deficiency is assessed, or to the thirtieth day after the filing of a waiver of the right to file a petition with the Board of Tax Appeals, whichever date is the earlier, and, in addition, 5 per cent of the amount of the deficiency if due to negligence or intentional disregard of rules and regulations without intent to defraud, or 50 per cent of amount of deficiency if due to fraud.

Income

Salaries.—Enter as Item 1 all salaries, wages, or other compensation received from outside sources by (a) yourself, (b) your husband or wife if a joint return is filed, and (c) each dependent minor child.
Interest.—Enter as Item 2 all interest received or credited to your account during the year on bank deposits, notes, mortgages, and corporation bonds, except interest on bonds containing a tax-free covenant which should be entered as Item 2(a) if you filed the ownership certificate on Form 1000A claiming exemption. The tax of 1½% paid by the debtor corporation on such interest should be entered as Item 18. Interest on bonds is considered income when due and payable.
Dividends.—Enter as Item 3 the amount received as dividends on stock of domestic corporations, including your share of such dividends on stock owned by a partnership, or an estate or trust.
Other Income.—Enter as Item 4 all other taxable income, including dividends on stock of foreign corporations, income of an estate or trust, and your share, whether received or not, in the profits of a partnership.

Deductions

Taxes.—Enter as Item 6 all personal taxes and taxes on property paid during the year. Do not include Federal income taxes, taxes imposed upon sales by the manufacturer, nor taxes assessed against local benefits to your property.
Contributions.—Enter as Item 7 any contributions or gifts made during the year to any corporation or fund organized and operated exclusively for religious, charitable, or educational purposes. The amount claimed shall not exceed 15 per cent of the net income computed without the benefit of this deduction. The names of organizations and amounts so distributed to each in space above.
Other Deductions.—Enter as Item 8 any other deductions authorized by law, including interest paid on personal indebtedness.

NOTE.—If you are engaged in a profession or business, including farming, use Form 1040, regardless of amount of income.

INDEX

CPSIA information can be obtained at www.ICGtesting.com
Printed in the USA
BVOW07s1750230216

437701BV00004B/5/P